爆 · 蛹

王昊然 Wang Haoran

英文翻譯：張菁
English Translation: Gigi Chang

BLAST

NEW WORK 新創作
香港藝術節委約及製作
Commissioned & produced by the Hong Kong Arts Festival

前言

舞台可投射自我最優及最劣一面,反映出令人愉悅或沮喪的影像,還提供我們不懂但卻可即時理解的觀點。這是它的魅力所在。

第41屆香港藝術節兩部最新劇作 —《爆蛹》及《屠龍記》將這份舞台獨有的懾人魅力發揮得淋漓盡致,兩劇包含多角度的對立觀點:內省外窺。作為觀眾的我們,將所有層出不窮的面向串連起來,真相逐步揭盅。

今年推出的第三部新作為室內歌劇《蕭紅》的文本,筆觸溢滿詩意、抒情及細膩情懷,透過蕭紅文學作品所啟迪的靈感,帶出這位出色女作家的生平及作品的全新觀感。

自2009年起,藝術節每年製作、巡演及出版本地全新劇作,直到2012年,共推出144場由香港藝人創作的本地戲劇作品,於本地、中國及亞洲其他地區上演。

特別要感謝多年來與我們並肩努力的藝人,以及於2013年與藝術節合作的藝術夥伴。我亦衷心感謝香港藝術節團隊,讓我以身為其中一份子而感到自豪。還要藉此感謝一直給我源源啟迪的藝術盟友,讓我透過優秀表演節目領略其獨特的奇妙魅力。

何嘉坤
香港藝術節行政總監

Foreword

The stage can show us the best and worst of ourselves, reflect images that delight or dismay, offer views that we may not know but can instantly recognise. That is its power.

Two new plays of the 41st HKAF, *Blast* and *Smear*, exploit this unique capacity, and encompass opposing views in multiple dimensions: looking in, looking out, reflecting reflections to look at how each sees others and are seen by them in turn, while we the audience, complicit in all possible perspectives, watch the action unfold.

A third new work published this year is the libretto for the chamber opera *Heart of Coral*. Poetical, lyrical and richly nuanced, it draws upon the literary source that inspired this new work, and offers new perspectives on the life and works of this remarkable woman and outstanding writer.

144 performances of new works by Hong Kong's creative talent have been presented at home, elsewhere in China and farther afield in the region between 2012 and 2009, when the HKAF first embarked on producing, publishing and touring new local work to premier in each Festival.

I am immensely grateful to the artists who have worked with us through these years, and to the artists who form or renew an association with the HKAF in 2013. I look forward to doing more with them in the years ahead. I am also deeply grateful to the HKAF team, who make me proud to be part of this organisation and who continue to inspire me to reflect upon the wonder and power of great performances.

Tisa Ho
Executive Director, Hong Kong Arts Festival

編劇的話

文：王昊然

一天，香港藝術節辦公室的姑娘阿宛找到我，希望我寫一篇編劇的話，我欣然答應了。

兩個月過後，我仍一字未動。實在想不到該寫什麼，於是我翻開了以前所看演出的場刊，我要參考參考，其他編劇究竟寫了些什麼。

我把近兩年香港新劇作的場刊都翻了個遍：鄭國偉、黃詠詩、意珩、李穎蕾、莊梅岩、潘惠森、陳敢權、杜國威。都是活躍於劇壇一線的編劇，其中不乏大名者。

我仍不知該如何下筆。

我想起我家花園住着一位哲學家，每次見到我，他都要問：

"你是誰？"

"你從哪裡來？"

"你到哪裡去？"

這實在是三條哲學難題。他是花園小區的保安，我久居香港，每次回深圳都沒有人認得我。

就如現在居住在香港一樣，作為一名編劇，沒有觀眾認得我。而香港藝術節居然不怕血本無歸用上了我的劇本，在此不得不佩服藝術節與蘇國雲先生的魄力。

這是我首部正式公演的劇作，沒能在大陸登台，卻在熟悉又陌生的香港亮相，香港這個社會的包容度實在出乎我意料。

初次見面，大概也會有人對我提出那三條難題吧。

關於第一問，這本說明書應該有補充。

關於第二問，應該也有。

至於何去何從，實在不是我說了算吶。

王昊然

生於湖南，長在深圳，居於香港。編劇作品包括《桎梏》、《叉燒》、《森林海中的紅樓》等，導演作品包括《作家之死》、《焦灼的女人》、《菲德拉的愛》等，主演劇目包括《威尼斯商人》、《浮石傳》、《金尾小恐龍》等。曾獲深圳大學英語文學學士（輔修日語），香港演藝學院戲劇藝術碩士（優異）。

Playwright's Note

Text: Wang Haoran

One day, Yuen from the Hong Kong Arts Festival contacted me. She hoped I could write the Playwright's Note. I happily agreed.

After two months, I still hadn't written a word. I really couldn't think of anything to write, so I flicked through the house programmes of all the performances I have seen. I wanted to see what others had written.

I looked through programmes of every new play from Hong Kong in the last two years: Cheong Kwok-wai, Wong Wing-sze, Yan Yu, Lee Wing-lui, Chong Mui-ngam, Poon Wai-sum, Anthony Chan and Raymond To. They are all playwrights active at the forefront of theatre, and some are rather famous.

I still didn't know where to start.

I thought of the philosopher that stations in the garden of the residential compound where my family live. Every time he sees me, he asks:

"Who are you?"

"Where did you come from?"

"Where are you going?"

These are three truly difficult philosophical questions. He is the compound's security. Since I live in Hong Kong, whenever I return to Shenzhen, no one recognises me.

Just like how I am living in Hong Kong right now. As a playwright, no audience recognises me. Yet the Hong Kong Arts Festival does not fear that they may not recoup a penny by taking my play; I cannot but show my admiration for the courage of the Festival and Mr So Kwok-wan.

This is my first formal stage production. It did not make it to the stage in the mainland, but is debuting in the both familiar and alien Hong Kong. The Hong Kong society's inclusivity has exceeded my expectations.

At our first meeting, those three difficult questions may well be raised.

As for the first question, this book should have the information.

As for the second one, should be included here also.

As for what's next, well, my words don't really count.

Wang Haoran

Born in Hunan, Wang Haoran grew up in Shenzhen and now lives in Hong Kong. His plays include *The Shackle*, *The Barbecued Pork* and *The Red Mansion in the Immense Forest*. His directorial credits include *The Death of a Writer*, *The Anxious Women* and *Phaedra's Love*. His acting credits include *The Merchant of Venice*, *The Tale of a Floating Stone* and *The Little Dinosaur with a Golden Tail*. He received a Master in Playwriting from the HKAPA and a Bachelor in English Literature (minoring Japanese) from Shenzhen University.

《爆蛹》首演於第 41 屆香港藝術節，
2013 年 3 月 8 日，香港文化中心劇場
Blast premiered at the Studio Theatre, Hong Kong Cultural Centre,
8 March, 2013, 41st Hong Kong Arts Festival

編劇 Playwright
王昊然 Wang Haoran

導演 Director
陳曙曦 Chan Chu-hei

佈景設計 Set Designer
賴妙芝 Yoki Lai

服裝設計 Costume Designer
余逢傑 Yue Fung-kit

燈光設計 Lighting Designer
馮國基 Fung Kwok-kee Gabriel

製作經理 Production Manager
張向明 Cheung Heung-ming

監製 Producer
香港藝術節 Hong Kong Arts Festival

角色及首演演出
Characters and Premiere Cast

大波
Dabo   陳永泉
             Chan Wing-chuen

小波
Xiaobo   王維
             Wang Wei

微波
Weibo   文傑聰
             Man Kit-chung

小琳
Xiaolin   周若楠
             Zhou Ruonan

封面照片：（由左至右）文傑聰、陳永泉、王維
Cover photographs: (from left to right)
Man Kit-chung, Chan Wing-chuen, Wang Wei

《爆．蛹》簡介

一個正在不斷遷拆不斷重建的城市，

一處堅尼系數超標的貧困城中村，

三個孤獨的三無宅男，

擠在一個沒有過去沒有明天的劏房，

他們從廁所的哲學辯論開始，

掀起一場荒謬絕倫的精子保衛戰，

南腔北調，各出奇謀，

情節出人意表，笑出眼淚。

【人　物】

王大波－披薩送貨員，48 歲。
王小波－某產品銷售員，32 歲。
王微波－某公司文員，25 歲。

注：大波只説粵語，能聽懂普通話；
　　小波只説普通話，粵語不佳 [説粵語時，以（粵）註明]；
　　微波兩種語言皆可 [説普通話時，以（普）註明]。

* 含不雅但生活化用語
「/」代表下一句對白的起始位置。
「－」代表本句對白被下一句對白打斷的位置。

第 一 幕

【任何一個快速崛起的城市】

【鴻坑村，或是任何一條有待拆除重建的城中村】

【一所破舊的出租公寓內】

【一間廁所，一個起居室，僅此而已】

【起居室內，貼着三堵牆依次擺放着小波（左）、大波（中）和微波（右）的床，兩邊的床有床簾遮擋。中間的牆有扇小窗，窗邊有一張飛鏢靶，上面插着三支鏢。牆壁高處掛着一個時間極不穩定的鐘】

【廳中央有一張陳舊的茶几，兩張凳子。茶几上擺放着煙灰缸、杯子和一卷手紙】

【不斷從窗外傳來建築工地的轟隆聲，時鐘的指針隨着打樁節奏一格一格往下掉】

【微波和大波】

【大波正在整理行裝準備出門，微波坐在床沿】

大： 房東話等對面棟樓打完樁就輪到呢度架喇。

微： 嘩唔好扯開話題先，其實我明白你感受嘅大佬。

大： 咩感受啫？我唔明咩 / 感受喎。

微： 即係，嘩，我都知仆街係咩一回事嘅 –

大： 咩啊，咩仆街呀。

微： 唔係……跌親、跌親，其實你年紀唔細架喇 –

大： 我好老咩宜家？

微： 唔係，即係……啲嘢壞咗唔緊要 –

大： 壞？咩壞吖？壞咩吖？

微： 個馬桶。

大： 哦，壞咗呀？ –

微： 係。

大： 哦。

微： 個馬桶 –

大： 得架喇、得架喇，細佬我仲趕住送披薩吖。

微： 個馬桶壞咗唔緊要 –

大： 得架喇！呢啲嘢用耐咗係好易舊架喇！ –

微： 唔係，唔係用耐咗嘅問題 –

大： 咁即係咩呀？ –

微： 即係你唔好企喺個馬桶上邊屙屎呀！

【強而有力的打樁聲將二人的對話淹沒】

【小波上，雙手捲成望遠鏡望向窗外】

【對面磨砂窗後，彷彿有一個女人的身影】

【聲音變得朦朧一片，時間也彷彿靜止了一般，只有她迷人的雙腿在流動】

【女人下】

【小波和大波】

【小波給大波按摩，大波發出舒服的呻吟】

大： 係、係、係呢個位！

小： 這個穴位，如果再大力一點⋯⋯

大： 啊⋯⋯啊⋯⋯正⋯⋯

小： 老大你看過《我愛錢》這本書嗎？

大： 書？⋯⋯啊⋯⋯我字都唔識隻⋯⋯喔⋯⋯啊⋯⋯

小： 《我愛錢》，台灣的，知道吧？

大： 啊⋯⋯知⋯⋯好撚多奶茶鋪架嘛⋯⋯啊⋯⋯

小： 「有錢的人未必懂得借錢，會借錢的人未必沒有錢。有些人就是通過借錢成功地建立了人脈，愈借愈有錢！」

大： 啊⋯⋯

小： 假如對方經常按時還錢，還有人不信他嗎？就好比說，我，老大你難道不信我嗎？

大： ⋯⋯啊！啊！啊！！！

【響起了大悲咒的音樂】

【微波一人，在打坐】

微： 觀自在菩薩 行深般若波羅蜜多時
照見五蘊皆空 度一切苦厄
舍利子 色不異空 空不異色
色即是空 空即是色
⋯⋯
色即是空 空即是色
⋯⋯
色即是空 空即是色
⋯⋯

【大悲咒淡去】

【小波出現在一旁】

【微波和小波】

小： 我總覺得自己欠女人太多。

微： 色即是空，空即是色......

小： ......你不懂，你都沒有過愛情怎麼會懂？

微： ......

小： 她身上有種純真，讓我無地自容......

【磨砂窗後，一名打扮樸素的女子輕輕走出】

小： 她的臉像出水的芙蓉，笑聲如銀鈴清脆，她就像一杯清澈的泉水，你什麼都看不到，卻美得很，簡單得很，很簡單，很簡單，簡單得就想喝掉它那麼簡單。

【女子消失】

小： 可我們一年只能見幾次，我每次去湖北只能是陪她和她爸賣香蕉......我覺得很孤獨很無助，就不知道自己要幹什麼。

微： 你有冇去過對面嘅髮廊？

小： 髮廊？

微： 我識個女仔，係嗰度幫啲客洗頭。介紹你識吓？

【窗外傳來打樁聲，令牆上時鐘的針搖晃不斷】

【公寓內】

【大波與微波】

【微波準備出門上班，邊忙邊說】

微：　大佬，你今日有冇用洗手間？

大：　……有。

微：　有冇開大？

大：　唔關我事架 −

微：　唔關你事？

大：　細佬，呢次真係唔關我事，我今日送完披薩返嚟一打開廁所門就見到 −

微：　大佬，我呢個人係有啲潔癖，首先我要 say sorry，超 sorry，我係個麻煩人 −

大：　得架喇、得架喇，將就下咁用喇 −

微：　就？……大佬，呢啲嘢我就唔到架喎……

大：　真係唔明點解我哋要用馬桶呢一種工具！ −

微：　你知唔知我揩到晒啲嘢呀！搞到我對手……唉！我仲未食早餐架！

【微波下，大力甩門】

【時間已經是下午】

【大波與小波】

【小波拉開床簾走出來，拿起桌上的抹手紙走進洗手間】

大：　記得整乾淨個馬桶呀。

【洗手間傳來小波的聲音，伴隨如廁時的呼吸聲】

小：　我什麼時候沒弄乾淨了？

16

大：　你今朝冇用過咩？

小：　問這個幹嘛喇？

大：　冇，細佬今朝問我點解你用完之後唔整乾淨啫。

小：　問你？為什麼不直接來問我？

大：　問吓啫，你唔喺度呀嘛。你用過嚟呀？

小：　沒啊，我早上不拉屎的。

【大波下】

【同一地點，時間已是晚上，公寓內一片漆黑】

【微波進門】

【突然響起小波的聲音，微波明顯受到驚嚇】

小：　以後關於我的事你直接問我。

微：　黐線做咩唔開燈？

【小波點了一根煙，黑暗中只見一點火光】

小：　你早上為什麼問老大我有沒上廁所？

微：　（普）我沒問啊。

小：　你沒問？

微：　（普）對啊，我只問他有沒有用。

小：　他用了嗎？

微：　（普）沒有。你用了嗎？

小：　……

【打椿聲消失】

【深夜】

【公寓的洗手間內】

【大波一人】

【大波注視着面前的馬桶，緊夾着兩腿，約有半分鐘。他深吸了一口氣，脫下褲子，坐了上去。他憋足了全身力氣，臉漲得通紅，還是拉不出。他立起身來，掀起馬桶坐墊，嘗試用腳踮了踮馬桶，確定不會塌，他提起腳，猶豫了一下，又縮了回來，他抽出衛生紙擦了擦馬桶上的腳印。隨後，他彎下腰把鞋子脫掉，準備赤腳踩上去。他又猶豫了一下，他從紙筒抽出許多衛生紙，鋪在地上，接着往前一跨一蹲，動作非常自然、非常順暢、非常自信。在蹲下的那一瞬間，他非常愉快】

【小波的床上】

【小波一人，對着他床前一張沙灘美女海報】

小：「大家久等了！下面讓我們以最熱烈的掌聲歡迎我們的上線、我們的偶像、我們的導師 ─ 王總，王小波先生！」
　　『（鼓掌）啪啪啪啪！（停頓）我親愛的夥伴們！你們好嗎？！』
　　「好！很好！非常好！Yeah！」
　　『我們都要很愛很愛對方！很愛很愛我們的朋友！你們說好不好？！』
　　「好！很好！非常好！Yeah！」
　　『（溫柔地）那我提議你們給身邊的朋友一個最真誠最真誠的擁抱。好不好？！』
　　「好！很好！非常好！Yeah！」
　　『（擁抱狀）今晚我王某一定能幫助你們找到自己！找到方向！找到生命的意義！讓我們一起奮鬥，一起成功，你們說好不好？』

【微波的床上】

【響起大悲咒的音樂】

微： ......
舍利子 色不異空 空不異色
色即是空 空即是色
......
色即是空 空即是色
......
色即是空 空即是色
......

【「啪！」地一聲】

家下有兩把刀，你一把，我一把，今日件事就喺度解決唔好俾
佢出街！

【停頓】

【微波深吸一口氣，繼續打坐】

【大悲咒淡去】

【窗外轟隆作響】

【小波和大波】

【小波高舉手中的手機】

小： 我為什麼不吃不喝不賭不嫖花五千塊買個愛鳳？！

大： ......

小： 老大，你......知不知道你最大的缺陷是什麼？

大： ......

小：　自信，你沒自信。

大：　……

小：　你知不知道一個男人最不能沒有的是什麼？

大：　……

小：　自信！

大：　……

小：　比如說裏邊那個被你蹲壞了的馬桶，你為什麼要蹲它？為什麼不坐它？為什麼你就不能接受這個大都市的新事物？因為你不自信。

大：　……

小：　又比如說，房東這兩棟樓總值九千萬，而你，卻只能租！請問你和房東的差別到底在哪？難道你們的智商真他媽相差有幾千倍嗎？有嗎？有木有？！

大：　冇 –

小：　那差別到底在哪兒？哪兒？！

大：　自信 –

小：　Very good！Very good！老大，你的自信開始慢慢培養了。那，怎樣才能培養自信？

大：　……

小：　首先必須把自己當做一塊招牌！

大：　……

小：　在這個時代你沒等別人發現就已經錯失良機一落千丈！所以呢，所以什麼？！所以咩？！

大： 招牌 –

小： 沒錯！招牌！所以……你沒愛鳳就說明你思想有問題啊。

大： ……

小： （粵）知唔知咩係搖一搖？

大： ……搖一搖？

【小波搖一搖手中的 iPhone，社交軟件微信發出一個提示音】

【小波展示給大波看】

小： （粵）（冷靜地）咁咪有條女囉。

【停頓】

小： 所以，愛鳳，不僅僅是愛鳳，還是……還是什麼？

大： 一部電話 –

小： 還是生活、自信、尊嚴、地位、品位、風度、氣場、內涵，所有的一切！

大： ……

小： 男人可以一無所有，卻必須有個愛鳳，即使不抽不喝不賭不嫖也他媽必須有一個最閃亮的愛鳳 –！

【小波下】

【大波走近微波】

【大波和微波】

大： 如果我有單生意。

【微波沒有理會】

大：　如果單生意有一百萬。

【微波沒有理會】

大：　如果我搵埋你一齊玩。

【微波還是沒有理會】

大：　喂……喂……睇緊咩？

微：　報紙。

【停頓】

大：　報紙度寫啲咩吖？

微：　新聞。

大：　新聞度講啲咩吖？

微：　頭條。

大：　頭條寫左啲咩吖？

微：　跳樓。

大：　有人跳樓？點解？

微：　可以上報紙。

大：　憑咩吖？

微：　憑佢跳樓。

大：　唔跳唔得咩？

微：　唔跳樓就冇人睇，冇人睇冇新聞，冇新聞冇意思，人生冇晒意思不如去死，橫掂都死不如跳樓死。

大：　哦。

微： 所以有樓嘅地方一定有人跳。你估對面起緊棟 building 咁高俾人住架? 俾人跳架!

大： Buil......

微： 樓 –

大： 啊我知 –

微： 唎,呢個學生哥幾識揀樓吖。

大： 學生都跳?

微： 呢排全世界都考緊 U 呀嘛。

大： U......

微： 大學 –

大： 吖我知,你都考過?

微： 梗係啦。

大： 考到咗?

【停頓】

微： 嗯。

大： 咁你畢業係咪有個學位架?

微： 嗯。

大： 咁你個學位係咪有張證架?

微： 嗯。

大： 咁張證書可唔可以借我望下架?

微： 八點半,夠鐘返工!

【微波出門】

【隱隱傳來打樁聲，伴隨着一股迷離又憂傷的旋律】

【大波一人】

【遠處走過一名學生模樣的女子】

大：　女！

【女子停】

大：　係咪女？
　　　……

大：　你玩咩失蹤？
　　　……

大：　你係咪考唔到學校？
　　　……

大：　唔讀書唔會死架。
　　　……

大：　你考咗三年喇。
　　　……

大：　你仲想點？
　　　……

大：　你想出國？
　　　……

大：　出國真係咁好？
　　　……

大：　你係咪覺得老豆唔多掂？
　　　……

大： 你係咪覺得老豆好唔掂？

【女子下】

大： 喂！喂！

【大波追前，下】

【小波進門，將門大力關上】

小： 我不明白誒，利用你？我今晚不過讓你幫我搬了幾箱貨就利用你了？

微： （普）我說的不是搬東西的事。

小： 那你說的是什麼？我出差才回來，跟你什麼接觸都沒有，然後就收到短信說我利用你，我搞不懂誒。

微： （普）你有沒看清楚我 SMS 上問你什麼？

小： 你問了什麼？除了說我利用你你還說了什麼？

微： （普）我問你有沒有把我當過朋友。

【小波電話響】

小： 喂，爸，一會兒打給你。

【小波掛電話】

小： 你當然是我朋友，我跟很多朋友都說你是我最好的兄弟，你可以問。

微： （普）我想你還沒弄懂我的意思。

小： 那麻煩你普通話講好一點，你說你到底什麼意思？

微： 我……你可以去睇本書，叫……《不要控制我》，好唔錯。

【小波電話響】

【小波關機】

小： 微波，我們現在先不談書，你就說，你什麼意思。

微： 我……

小： 說啊！

微： 我……其實……

小： 你自己都不知道！

微： 你可唔可以冷靜啲？！

【停頓】

小： 你說。

【停頓】

微： （普）我……我覺得，你只是把我當成一種投資。

小： 什麼？

微： 我覺得你將 friend 當成一種投資。

小： 投資？

微： ……

小： 是啊，朋友不就是這樣的喔？我對你好點你對我好點，互相都希望得到點回報的喔？是啊，朋友就是種投資啊。

微： 你投……你投資咗我啲咩？你除咗日日食我嘅用我嘅你投資咗啲咩？

小： 噢，說白了就是覺得我虧欠了你嘛，不甘心！哎喲，我真搞不懂，當初給錢你不要，現在又來這一套！你什麼意思？

微： 大家都係搵兩餐，要咗你啲錢驚你諗埋一邊話我唔夠義氣啫！

小： 你現在就夠義氣？你現在指着我鼻子罵就很義氣了？口口聲聲兄弟兄弟，小算盤打得精得不得了！

微： 我打你咩算盤？我借錢俾你又介紹女仔你識，我打你咩算盤？

小： 嘖嘖嘖嘖，得了得了，話不要說得太白，你就是看着我吃你用你那幾個錢嘛，我給你，你說，究竟幾個錢？算清算楚，我全部出一半好不好？！

微： 你當我咩？我微波差嗰幾舊錢咩？

小： 那我就搞不懂了，你到底什麼意思？

微： 你冇領我嘅情。

小： 什麼？

微： 你……我……唉……我……

小： 王微波我告訴你，我從來就沒有欠你什麼！

微： ……

小： 是就是！不是就不是！你能不能不要徘徊於是與不是之間！我告訴你，我小波不是這樣的人！我小波不是借錢不還、愛佔便宜的小人！明白嗎？！今天公司一大堆破事已經讓我快崩潰了你知道嗎？！你這樣讓我很辛苦！為什麼跟你相處比談戀愛還要辛苦？我很累！我現在只想哭！我真的很累！

【沉默】

微： 好，我就問你一句。

小： 你說。

【停頓】

微： 你有冇真係當過我朋友？

【停頓】

小： 你是我最好最好最好的兄弟。

【停頓】

微： OK……OK。

【小波一人】

小： （對着電話）爸，我現在自己也欠了一屁股債，哪兒有錢借給你？不，爸，我……我哪句話有怪你的意思了？……爸你能不能好好說話，為什麼我們一講話就要吵？……是的是的，我不該去賭，我應該把錢全給你拿去炒股嘛！如果不是因為你賠光了我的錢，我怎麼會想着賭回來？……你……我無能？是的，我是無能……我是無能……我最最無能的就是做了你的兒子！我做了你的兒子！你總是影響我影響我影響我……不斷地影響我！我恨自己為什麼……為什麼那麼像你！我以為吧，出來闖了就可以……擺脫你，不會再有人來管我交什麼朋友、有什麼目標……但是，我沒辦法，我真的沒辦法，我愈活就愈覺得自己像足了你！表情、脾氣……就連說話的語氣也是！還有那些缺點！那些到處都是的缺點！我他媽自己都不能忍受的缺點！一個沒有用的敗類！你……知不知道，是你毀了我，是你毀了我的生活！

【第一幕完】

第 二 幕

【晚上八點多，公寓內】

【窗外傳來工地施工的轟隆聲，牆上的鐘仍舊不穩定】

【大波一人】

【桌上擺了一個九寸大小的披薩，已經少了半邊】

【旁邊擺着大波的手機，舊款單色諾基亞，手機不斷震動，良久】

【大波拿起手機往桌上一拍，手機停止震動】

【小波進，神情疲憊】

小：　老大。

【停頓】

【小波注意到披薩，走到大波旁邊】

【停頓】

【大波將披薩往前推】

小：　謝謝，我還真餓了。

【兩人低頭吃披薩】

小：　你還好吧?

【沉默】

【大波從桌底抽出一盒 12 寸大的披薩】

大：　食埋佢喇。

小：　忘記洗手了。

【小波進洗手間】

【大波的手機再次震動，許久】

【小波拿着書《不要控制我》出來】

【大波拿起手機往桌上一拍】

【桌上的手機第三次震動，大波反應迅速地拿起手機往桌上一拍】

【大波從桌底抽出厚厚一疊 12 寸大的披薩】

大： 食喇。

【停頓】

大： 你有冇興趣幫人生仔？

【停頓】

大： 有錢……

【手機震動】

【大波接通電話】

大： 講嘢。

【停頓】

大： 咩？

【停頓】

大： 我老友食緊。

【停頓】

大： 係吖我老友食緊你件海鮮芝士披薩啊。

【停頓】

大： 我知你要走海鮮，所以我老友咪幫你走撚晒佢囉。

【停頓】

大： 咩微信呀？我車到去火車站你先打俾我？咩呀？微…微乜春吖？

【停頓】

大： 係係係，你鍾意微信你冚家都微信，拜拜！

【停頓】

大： 咩係微信？

【小波拿出手機，搖一搖，社交軟件「微信」發出一個音效】

【停頓】

大： 繼續啦。

小： ……

大： 食晒佢，我請。

小： 我沒吃到這個有海鮮啊。

大： 你食緊呢件，我送到去火車站先收到電話要改海鮮芝士披薩，走芝士，等我再送到去佢又話要改海鮮芝士披薩，走海鮮！我騎咗一個鐘車！

【小波翻着旁邊的披薩】

小： 咦，防輻射披薩？

大： 呢件防輻射送去機場架，條友要去日本。

小： 防洗腦披薩？

34

大： 「（普）不好意思」，呢件唔啱你，你冇得挽架喇。

小： 每張披薩都要兩百多。

大： 宜家啲客，一唔撚爽就同我講：今時今日咁嘅服務態度點得架？！

小： 一二三四⋯⋯

大： 屌搵劉德華啊笨！

小： 十盒，兩千多塊錢⋯⋯

大： 一日九個鐘，出邊 40 度高溫，我揸住架電單車四圍咁轉，／就係為咗班咁嘅粉腸。

小： 其實為什麼要叫它披薩？

大： 然後返嚟收到我老婆從湛江打電話嚟話個女失咗蹤成個月，／我真係着咗。

小： 為什麼不是烙餅？

大： 失蹤成個月，我老婆佢竟然粒聲都唔響，我真係着咗。

小： 它們的差別到底在哪？

大： 着到我吖，痔瘡都多⋯⋯多⋯⋯多咗幾粒，仲要揸九個鐘車行勻全市，架電單車就嚟煎到我個屎忽九成熟喇。

【停頓】

【小波從包裹拿出一個銀色防曬坐墊】

小： 給。

大： 咩？

小： 防曬坐墊。

【停頓】

大： 多謝。

【停頓】

小： 我可能要搬。

大： 搬？去邊呀？

小： 不知道，我得換工作了，這樣下去會崩潰的。

大： 宜家啲人咁易崩潰嘅？

小： 我真想回去。

大： 返邊呀？

小： 我不知道。

大： 你仆心仆命先留低宜家話走就走？

小： 是我自己的問題，我有問題 –

大： 唔係唔係，我問你點解走啫。

小： 我好累，每天一下樓看見大街上那麼多人我就覺得累 –

大： 條街日日都多人架啦，你咪適應佢囉 –

小： 我適應五年了，我適應不了 –

大： 點會啫，我都得喇 –

小： 我真的不行，我不行 –

大： 有咩唔得吖？男人冇得話唔得！

小： 我不想適應！我不想適應！ OK？

大： 所以話呢個係你自己嘅問題！

小： 是啊，是啊，我剛剛就說是我自己的問題啊！

【沉默】

【小波搖一搖手機，社交軟件「微信」發出一個音效】

大： 你等錢洗？

【小波再搖手機，發出一個音效】

【小波第三次搖手機，發出一個音效】

大： 你等錢洗？

小： 去不去東莞？

【停頓】

大； 你等錢洗？

小： 去不去東莞？

【停頓】

大： 你等錢洗？

小： 是的我很想去但我沒錢。

【停頓】

大： 你 79 年架？

【小波走到一旁玩飛鏢】

大： 咁你即係 34 歲。

【停頓】

大： 你身份證上邊寫嘅都係 79 年?

【停頓】

大： 你咩血型?

【停頓】

大： 有冇性病?

【停頓】

大： 有冇愛滋?

【停頓】

大： 我手入邊有一份約，你……

小： 老大! 我現在真的很想去! 真的真的很想去! 我就不明白你為什麼不表個態!

【小波將手中三隻飛鏢同時奮力扔出，卻飛出了窗外】

【沉默】

小： 我已經很久沒休息了，老大，再問你最後最後一次，去不去?

大： ……

小： 我是這麼看的，不知道就等於沒有。

大： ……

小： 安全方面你放一萬個心，我那邊有人。

大： ……

小： 那邊可不比對面那些大姐，你去了就知道什麼叫 professional.

大： Pro……

小： 專業，專業，懂嗎？

【小波雙手捲成望遠鏡望向窗口對面】

【隱約出現一個女人的身影】

小： （激情四射地）男人，千古以來就一直就是歷史的主宰，而女
人，千古以來卻一直是男人的主宰。古人云：「何意百煉鋼，
化為繞指柔。」如果你是一個優柔寡斷、生性多疑的男人，那
麼你應該去四川，巴蜀女子直爽潑辣，猶如川劇的變臉，她們
的七情六欲都溢於言表，你的所見，即你的所得，無須捉摸、
無須猜忌，她們純真的性格總會為你指引正確的航向，除非你
剛愎自用。然而假如你是個剛愎自用的男人，你應該嘗一嘗上
海女人，你會發現自己終於不必再強裝一頭雄獅，而可以成為
一隻沒有自我、無憂無慮的吉娃娃，上海女人的精明幹練絕對
能讓你脫胎換骨、重獲新生，除非你自甘墮落。而假如你自甘
墮落，你應該去湖南，湖南女人會讓你明白：墮落是沒有止境
的。千萬不要嘗試刺探湖南女人的心事，她們遠看只是可愛的
紅辣椒，待你一口咬下，如舌頭着了數鞭，你便明白「無法自
拔」這四字的由來其實是「痛，並快樂着」，從她們身上你必
能領略何謂湘女多情、我見猶憐，除非你瞎了眼。而假如你真
的瞎了，人生暗淡無光、困惑迷茫，東莞歡迎你！因為在那兒
無須精挑細選，無須權衡利弊，只需準備人民幣。放眼大中華，
獨此一家，無論是四川、上海、湖南等等等等，縱橫南北，
開合古今，各地佳麗，百般武藝，盡在東莞不言中。古人云：
「回眸一笑百媚生，六宮粉黛在東莞。」古人云：「黃沙百戰
穿金甲，不到東莞終不還。」無論台灣還是香港乃至整個東南
亞，東莞都是男人們必須朝拜的聖地！不到東莞非好漢，屈指
行程一頓飯！

【小波扔出 iPhone】

【女子下】

【大波接住 iPhone 端詳】

小： 就在這。

大： 110公里 –

小： 不用看，我很熟。

大： 個幾鐘 –

小： 開車一小時就到，我們可以打的。

【停頓】

大： 你駛唔駛問下個細佬。

小： 問他幹嘛?

大： 佢有車牌。

小． 那有什麼用，他沒車 –

大： 我有。

小： 你的電單車?

大： 四個轆架。

小： 哪兒搞來的?

大： 我有個兄弟咁啱呢幾日返鄉下，車停咗喺度 –

小： 用得着、用得着，多大?

大： 好大 –

小： 啥車?

大： 豬欄車。

小： 有車好，可以帶出去過夜。

大： 又方便又慳錢 –

小： 他去的，他肯定去 –

大： 咁肯定？

小： 這老弟是大色狼。

大： 睇唔出嘅 –

小： 大色狼一般都看不出的。

大： 我驚佢比較有文化唔鍾意掂呢味嘢呀 –

小： 你不知道？大色狼一般都很有文化的。

大： ……

小： 給你看點東西。

【小波走到微波床邊，拉開他的床簾】

【微波的床井然有序，床邊的小書架擺滿了書，牆壁掛有一幅字「寧靜致遠」，字的周圍貼滿了剪報，都是一些名畫和藝術照。床頭有一長條廁紙卷拉着，上面用紅色筆大大地寫着「再偷窺死全家」】

【停頓】

小： 來，咱們來看看，看看他的牆上到底都貼着些什麼。這是什麼？一個男的，和一女的，脫得精光，男的還跪下來聞那女的……嘖嘖嘖嘖，淫蕩！……這是什麼？一群不穿衣服的大波妹和大屌男戲水，嘖嘖嘖嘖，真淫蕩！……這是什麼？兩個不男不女的傢伙，還互相捏……太淫蕩了！還有這個還有這個，我操我操，這個牛，這不是女人的……我操，太淫蕩了！超級淫蕩！最搞笑的是……最搞笑的是……「寧一靜一致一遠！」啊—哈—哈—哈！老大，老大，你見過這樣的沒？好 hi 寧靜，好 hi 致遠！哈哈哈哈……

【小波笑癱在地】

【微波面無表情地走進門，他的背包上插着三隻鏢】

【停頓】

大： 咦你今日唔係返工咩？

微： 好大陣煙觲（音：除）。

【微波從口袋拿出噴霧向空中噴了噴】

【微波經過自己床邊，停住】

【微波放下背包，拉上床簾，走進洗手間】

【小波拔下飛鏢按回飛鏢靶】

【微波出】

微： 大佬 –

大： 我冇用過架。

【停頓】

微： 有冇見到我漏咗喺洗手間嗰本書？

大： 書？

微： 本書名叫《不要控制我》。

小： 是這本嗎？

【微波拿，小波不給】

小： 笑一笑。

【微波搶，小波不給】

微： 給我。

小： 好喇好喇，瞧你那認真的。

【扔給微波】

小： 生活是一面鏡子小伙子。

微： ……

小： 你笑它就笑，多笑笑。

大： 嚟，細佬，飲杯水先。

【微波坐下】

大： 今日咁早返嘅？

小： 該不會是被炒了吧兄弟，哈哈！

【停頓】

微： 係吖係吖滿意未吖？！！！

【沉默】

【微波一人】

微： 平時我返到公司鬼影都冇隻，今日就見到成群人逼喺道門度，話嚟見工嘅。未等我坐低主任就叫咗我入去。佢話（普）：「你還年輕，即使業績不好我也會給你個機會。」我淨係個斟茶遞水嘅文員，我唯一要做嘅就係排好公司嘅內刊，每次印 30 份發俾所有員工，上面會報道公司嘅近況、leader 嘅演講。為咗份嘢靚啲，我會作首詩印喺封底。我問係咪我啲詩寫得唔掂，吖主任擰擰頭話我係個好詩人。我問佢話，得呢份內刊係我嘅 job，我何來業績可言？主任話：「所以說你業績不好。」我問主任何來業績可言，主任話：「所以說你業績不好。」我問主任何來業績可言，主任話：「那你走吧。」我想搵柒佢，

43

我擘大個口話:「你說的是什麼機會?」於是乎,我揸住紙筆行入嗰條又暗又窄嘅走廊,主任把聲傳咗出嚟:「先交卷的先面試。」霎時似有萬幾隻甲由係 Bong 牆度係咁飛係咁跳,冇幾耐條走廊靜晒,剩番我一個。然後我 feel 到有人拍咗下我膊頭話:「天黑了,回去吧。」我諗咗半分鐘,好似過咗半粒鐘咁,然後我又用咗半粒鐘諗 ── 投先究竟我喺度諗緊也呢?

【公寓內】

小:　你該立馬走人的。

微:　……

小:　想屌就屌,你幹嘛不屌他?

微:　……

小:　讀那麼多書居然不懂屌人?

【停頓】

小:　來,坐這,坐老大面前。老大你背過身去。

【大波背對着微波】

小:　想像一下,這就是你那老闆。閉上眼睛,想像一下……

微:　……

小:　Feel 一下,辦公室的 space,他的樣子,他的氣味……

微:　……

小:　在他公司幹了幾年?

微:　(普)……兩年。

小:　這兩年有給你加薪嗎?

微： （普）……有。

小： 多少?

微： （普）……五百。

小： 兩年五百，每年二百五。

微： ……

小： Do you know，（粵）對面樓啲姐姐平均一粒鐘賺幾多錢吖?

微： I don't know.

小： （粵）四舊水。想摁多次鐘你要儲兩年吖哥哥仔。

微： ……

小： 他對你怎樣?

微： （普）……不怎樣。

小： 不，他對你比對一條狗還不如呢。

微： ……

小： 他滿意你的工作嗎?

微： （普）不滿意。

小： 為什麼?

微： （普）他不喜歡我。

小： 不喜歡你什麼?

微： （普）寫詩。

【微波伸手，遞出一張紙，小波接過】

45

小：　「它本是荒漠上離群索居的羔羊，

　　　　又不是森林中玲瓏機智的灰狼，

　　　　為何要它離開那片故土，

　　　　來這深山裏找尋它的原鄉？」

微：　（普）他覺得我炫耀……

小：　他 — 嫉 — 妒 — 你。

微：　……

小：　他怎麼評價你的詩？

微：　（普）他說，真正一坨臭狗屎。

【停頓】

小：　真正一坨……

【停頓】

微：　（普）臭狗屎。

【停頓】

小：　對他罵一句你覺得最粗的粗口。

微：　……

小：　來，勇敢點。

【停頓】

微：　（普）你他媽的。

小：　弱爆了，再來。

微： ……

小： 說呀。

微： ……

小： 跟我說，你媽個逼。

微： （普）……你媽個逼。

小： 操你媽個臭逼。

微： （普）操你媽個臭逼。

小： 操你媽個臭逼你個婊子養的賤貨！

微： （普）操你媽個臭逼你個婊子養的賤貨。

小： Good try！再大聲點兒！

微： （普）操你媽個臭逼你個婊子養的賤貨！

小： Good try！ Good try！

微： 屌你老母個臭屄生你舊乜鳩撚嘢！（"屄"，粵語發音為 "Hai"）

小： （粵）冇得彈！

微： 我唔撚柒鳩屌你個含撚笨柒個老母個生滋甩毛爛臭化屄花柳白濁梅毒性冷係都唔撚柒得既！你媽屄我做撚咗四年，四年呀！日日都要對撚住你個屄樣，仲撚臭過我屋企養條狗個屄！你老味對住啲女人就喺度搖頭擺尾扮撚晒狗叫，我想加少少人工你就捉我來開屄！我仆你個街屄面就愈來愈撚快！搞埋啲乜撚 project 就愈來愈鳩廢！請埋啲乜撚碩士以為好撚巴閉！出埋啲乜撚面試題仲難過屌屄！（潮州話）Por Nia Mo 你唔駛食飯嘅！Por Nia Mo 含撚就飽架喇！你老母屄！你老母個臭屄！你老母屄！臭屄！臭屄！臭屄！臭屄！臭屄！！！

【微波呼吸紊亂，像哮喘發作一樣，漸漸平復】

【較長沉默】

微：　……Sorry。

大：　……

【微波喝了兩口水】

微：　……有冇煙?

【大波遞煙】

【小波幫微波點煙】

【大波自己也點了一支煙】

【微波吸第一口嗆到】

【微波第二口把煙吸到嘴裏含着，忽地一下吐出】

【微波把煙丟進煙灰缸，含了一口水，咕嚕兩下吐進煙灰缸】

小：　兩年前，我們第一次在這個小房間認識，那晚我說過一句話，
　　　有誰還記得?！

【停頓】

大：　想去搵鐘?

【停頓】

小：　我還送了你們一人一張卡片。

微：　噢。

小：　你記得?！

大：　噢! 嗰晚我哋買咗成抽酒上天台度!

小： 你也記得？！

大： 你未俾錢添好似……

小： 我把那句話寫在了一張卡片上。

微： 我仲留着。

小： 在哪？

微： 黐喺牆度。

【小波快步拉開微波床位的簾子，「再偷窺死全家」六個字再次躍入眼前】

【小波扯下「再偷窺死全家」】

【小波在牆上尋找卡片】

【微波走上前拿下卡片，拉上簾子】

微： 「盡情書寫你的七彩人生，不必害怕……」

小： 「不必害怕，因為一切都可以擦掉重來，只要你願意，你相信。

【沉默】

小： 你們相不相信？

【沉默】

小： 實話說我今天去賭了，賭掉了我半年的積蓄，可是，我突然想起兩年前居然說過一句這樣的話！

【沉默】

小： 我還說過，我要創立自己的家族企業，（粵）我要改變呢個社會！

【停頓】

小： 你也說過！你說要成為大文豪！

微： （敏捷地）我冇咁講過。

小： 老大！你也有！

大： 咩？送少啲披薩？

小： 你說要讓女兒有書讀。

大： 係？

小： 這是一個最好的時代，一切都在重新開始，你們有沒有發現？

【停頓】

小： 只要你願意，你相信！

【停頓】

小： 所有的一切，都是嶄新的。就像窗外房東那棟樓，還有這鴻坑村裏裏外外的住宅 —— 拆除！然後重建！

【全體感動】

大： 咁你真係要聽下我嗰份約，大茶飯……

小： 今晚去喝酒！／我們好好計劃一下將來！

大： 係關於一個醫學實驗 –

微： 咁我淨係飲少少 –

大： 酒一定要飲嘅 –

小： 走，去東莞！

【停頓】

大： 咁快……

微： （普）東莞?

小： 是的，東莞。

微： （普）去搞什麼?

小： （粵）搞女人。

【停頓】

微： （普）你去?

小： 去啊。

【停頓】

微： （普）你……真的去?

小： 真去。

【停頓】

微： 你哋去啦。

小： 你不去?

微： 嗰啲嘢唔啱我。

大： 嘩，唔好急，俾時間你考慮下。

小： 靠，上個月說起去東莞的事你笑那麼開心以為我沒看出來嗎?

微： 係，上次聽你講性工作者啲嘢我係有笑，但我同你哋嘅笑／係唔一樣架。

小： 叫雞就叫雞，什麼找性工作者。你說，你的笑有什麼不一樣? 有什麼特別迷人的地方?

微： 我冇話迷人 −

小： 你的語氣就是這樣，連笑一下都比我們高級。

大： 細佬，如果你有咩苦衷可以講架 −

小： 你個逼就壓抑吧，跳樓得了，咧，就這，別跳遠了死在房東工
地上還得賴我們。

微： 我笑，係因為睇到一種 — 悲哀。

小： 啥？

微： 我憐憫你哋。

【停頓】

大： 吓？

小： 憐憫？憐憫誰，那些雞？

微： 你哋都值得憐憫。

【停頓】

大： 嗱，細佬，我知你辭咗份工有少少困難嘅，咁啦，你去嘅話我
請。

【停頓】

大： 點嘛？

小： ……

大： （對小波）請埋你。

【沉默】

大： 點嘛？

【沉默】

小： 你個逼還磨蹭什麼啊？！

大： 好喇，唯有搵第個兄弟揸車喇。

微： 揸車？

大： 兄弟借嘅。唔緊要，我尊重你。

【停頓】

微： 你搵唔到人揸車？

大： 係。

微： 如果真係，我可以幫下手。

大： 你去得？

微： 我想兜下風，散下心。

小： 我那邊有人，安全方面放一萬個心。

大： 咁你去了喔？

微： 如果你真係搵唔到人開車 –

大： 我搵唔到 –

微： 咁我去。

【停頓】

小： 快快快，收拾收拾，現在過去還趕得上第一撥！

大： 我有件事要同大家宣佈 –

【小波往茶几底下翻找一些東西】

小： 微波，前些天我切了橙子把刀放這下邊，你看到過嗎？

微： ……你要刀幹嘛？

小： 帶上，以防萬一。

大： 我有件事要同大家宣佈！

【停頓】

大： 好事嚟嘅。

【停頓】

大： 如果今晚搞掂佢，我一定請，幾次都無問題。

【停頓】

小： 搞不定呢？

大： 一定搞得掂，只要你願意，你相信。

小： 說吧老大。

【停頓】

大： 我手入面有份約 –

小： 什麼約？

大： 聽我講，前排凌晨我送披薩返嚟，半路有個人影同我揮手，話截唔到的，想我送佢一程。咁路上傾下先知原來佢係咩婦產科醫學研究所嘅所長，其實我心諗，夜媽媽一個人佢唔驚我危險架咩……咁我哋傾下傾下……佢隻手就擺咗落去我下面……

微： 坐得所長個位，個女人都應該幾大年紀了喔。

大： 男人嚟架。

54

小： 講重點。

大： ……我話：「你對手咁唔聽話，我點揸車吖。」佢又唔出聲。

小： 重點，老大。

大： 跟住佢講（普）：「給你一百萬，陪我一晚。」隨手就拎咗張
信用卡出嚟……當其時我諗：哇，黐線架。

小： 你該不會要我們做鴨吧。

大： 唔通堅嘅？但我真係下唔到決心。

小： ……

大： 走嗰陣時佢俾咗張卡片我話（普）：「看你這麼老實，這裏有
份合同，簽了到研究所來找我，可以賺不少的。」

【沉默】

大： 事情經過就係咁。

【停頓】

小： 重點！老大你說話完全沒有重點！

大： 份約簽咗賺一百萬。

【沉默】

【小波點煙，吸了一口】

【微波拿出噴霧噴了噴】

【小波走到窗口繼續抽煙】

小： 說，什麼合約，做鴨我不去。

大： 捐精呀。

小： ......

微： ......

大： 我講嘅係捐精。

【停頓】

大： 個研究所要做個一胎五仔五女嘅實驗，咁個實驗需要有條佬俾啲精佢哋，就係咁簡單。

【停頓】

微： 咁就一百萬？

大： 關於筆錢我係咁諗嘅......

小： 撒個尿。

【小波進洗手間】

大： ......單生意係我搵到嘅，咁我想自己輕鬆啲，又可以幫到你哋，所以如果你哋邊個簽咗佢，我分佢五成。

微： 五成？

大： 五成。

微： 50 萬？

大： 50 萬。

【小波出來，將手中的杯子往桌上一放】

小： 50 萬，成交。

【停頓】

【微波向前傾，掩鼻】

微：　你……

小：　沒錯。

微：　隻杯你刷牙用架嘛?

大：　嗱，小波……

【停頓】

大：　個杯呢就好撚多菌嘅，人哋做實驗唔會要。你啲嘢還番俾你。

【大波將杯子推回小波面前】

【小波用紙巾擦乾淨杯子】

微：　咁啦，大佬，不如你講吓候選人嘅條件，再睇睇我哋邊個啱啲，
　　　好唔好?

小：　我無所謂的呀。

【停頓】

小：　但是，我說假如啊，假如咱倆的候選條件不相上下，那怎麼
　　　辦?

微：　咁咪大佬決定囉。

【停頓】

小：　那不如直接讓老大決定好了，對不對?

微：　我咁公平啲。

【停頓】

小：　你說呢老大?

大：　……

微： 你驚咩吖？

小： 說我啊？我有什麼好怕的啦？你怕什麼？

大： 其實呢……

【停頓】

大： 你哋兩個都唔錯……

【停頓】

大： 一個有文化，又有骨氣……

【停頓】

大： 一個有自信，又靚仔……

【停頓】

大： 大家都係老友……

【停頓】

大： 所以……

【停頓】

大： 我希望你哋兩個……

【停頓】

大： 可以擺低成見……

【停頓】

大： 好好咁，傾一傾……

【沉默】

小： （對微波）你先說，你怕什麼？

大： 喂⋯⋯

微： 我可以驚啲咩？你驚嘅我都唔驚。

小： 好，請你告訴我，我怕什麼？

微： 你自己唔知架咩？

小： 誅，微波，你敢不敢像個男人？媽的跟娘們兒一樣。

大： 喂⋯⋯

微： 我警告你抹乾淨把口 –

小： OKOK，對不起，我的錯，我很誠懇地道歉，那我們好好地談
　　一談好不好？

【停頓】

微： 你話我驚，我一個大學畢業生驚你啲咩呢？

【停頓】

小： 噢，呵呵呵⋯⋯大學生，原來我是怕這個。老大你聽到沒有？
　　大學生！

大： ⋯⋯嗯。

小： 大學生，你現在多少錢一個月？

微： 唔關你事。

小： 也就幾千吧？我做傳銷月入兩萬時你在幹嘛？打醬油嗎？！

微： 咁你去住三房一廳嘅豪宅啊笨！

小： （粵）三房一廳唔算得咩豪宅曉唔曉吖？青頭仔！

大：　得得得！邊撚個都唔好簽，我自己簽，得未？！

小：　況且我一直都很懷疑你是不是大學生。

【沉默】

大：　……咁喇……啊細佬你簽咗佢。

小：　老大！

大：　然後嗰五成你哋自己分吖，你哋自己分，我唔撚得閒理你哋。

【大波走到一邊玩飛鏢】

【沉默】

小：　你簽還是我簽？

【停頓】

微：　咁你想點分？

小：　這樣，一、二、三、四、五……

【小波從茶几上的十份披薩中拿出五份，交給大波】

小：　你的老大，五成。

【大波繼續玩飛鏢】

【隨後，從茶几上的五份中抽出一份放在微波面前】

小：　一四分成。

微：　一四分。

小：　怎樣？

微：　簽咗拿四成？

小：　對，簽約的比較累。

微：　咁我簽？

【停頓】

小：　我和我爸都欠了一屁股債……

【停頓】

小：　前前後後……20 萬……

【停頓】

小：　這些天我老覺得有人跟蹤我……

【停頓】

小：　我真的不希望我的兄弟受到什麼牽連……

【小波抽多一份披薩放在微波面前（左二右三）】

小：　二三分成怎樣？

【停頓】

微：　其實我老豆醫病都好需要錢……

【停頓】

微：　不過我同大佬都識得照顧自己……

【停頓】

微：　你唔好諗太多……

【停頓】

微：　二三分成……我 OK 嘅……

【停頓】

小：　那……就這麼定了？二三分？

【微波從對面移出一份披薩放在自己面前】

微：　可以了。

【停頓】

小：　什麼意思？

微：　我簽。

【小波抽回一份疊在自己面前】

小：　那你只能分兩成。

微：　點解？

【停頓】

【小波點燃最後一支煙，把盒子捏扁了扔進垃圾桶，走到窗旁】

【微波拿出噴霧向空中噴了噴】

小：　老大，你說，現在怎麼辦？

大：　傾到邊吖？

小：　這樣，微波，咱倆誰都別爭，每人兩成半 –

微：　OK –

小：　兩成半啊，每人兩成半 –

微：　誰簽？

小：　誰愛簽誰簽！

微： 那你簽吧。

【停頓】

小： 可以！沒問題！我簽就我簽，我做人很爽快的。

【停頓】

小： 談妥了吧？

微： OK 的。

小： 談妥了我先下去買煙。

大： 搞掂喇？

【小波下，樓梯通道隱隱約約傳來他通電話的聲音:「喂，爸……」】

【聲音消失】

【微波拿過大波手中的飛鏢】

【停頓】

微： 你知唔知？

大： 我知。

微： 即係……大佬，你知唔知，我唔係歧視佢。

大： 我知我知。

微： 佢搵我笨，一次兩次有問題，friend 呀嘛，難免架……

大： Frien……

微： 朋友。

大： 我知。

微： 佢好醒架，表面功夫做到十足，又買宵夜又買底褲……你都收
　　過佢嗰條有超人公仔嘅底褲架係咪?

大： 係。

微： 我好 appreciate 佢呢啲促進友誼嘅行為……

大： Appre……

微： 感激。

大： 我知。

微： 但佢從來都唔會蝕大底，分分鐘搵你笨你唔知添。但我又好醒
　　喔! 次次都好清楚!

大： 你次次都俾佢搵到笨?

微： 因為我愛佢。

大： 吓?

微： 唔係……唔係嗰種愛……

大： ……

微： 我……

大： ……

微： 我覺得，佢俾到我要嘅嘢……

大： 吓?

微： 唔係……唔係嗰種嘢……我意思係……喺我最失落嘅時候，佢
　　可以幫到我。

大： 幫到咩?

微： 自信。

【停頓】

大： 噢。

微： 我成日覺得好孤獨好無助，我係一個脾氣太好嘅好人，但係其實有時我好羨慕佢，好想成為佢，可以咁直接，咁唔顧人哋感受……

大： 唔明。

微： 唔緊要，你唔駛明。

【微波走到飛鏢靶旁拔下飛鏢】

微： 其實我想講，我一直當佢兄弟，但佢當我水魚。佢開到聲，邊次我唔幫？佢想借錢，邊次我唔借？佢仲咁嚟對我？佢仲咁嚟對我？佢……我真係想啪兩把刀喺枱面話佢聽，你一把我一把，今日件事喺度解決，唔好俾佢出街！

【微波將三支飛鏢奮力插進靶心中】

【停頓】

大： 佢問你借錢？

微： 係。

大： 幾多錢？

微： 一千。

大： 還咗未？

微： 未，未到期，不過佢一般都準時嘅……

大： 佢都借咗我一千。

【小波上，一手拿着兩包煙，一手提着一袋啤酒】

小：　來，老大，你的煙！

微：　（普）這麼多酒？

小：　喝好了去幹女人呀。對不對啊老大？

大：　呵呵。

小：　難得今天這麼開心，來！

微：　（普）我不喝。

【小波拿出一支菊花茶】

小：　哈！菊花茶，來，下下火！

【小波開了兩瓶酒，遞給大波一瓶】

小：　老大，我先敬你。

【小波將一瓶酒一飲而盡，隨即又開了一瓶】

微：　……

大：　……

小：　我小波真正稱得上兄弟的就你們兩位。再敬你們，以後你們就
　　　是我親哥！

【小波喝完第二瓶酒，又開了一瓶】

大：　喂細佬你得唔得架。

【小波立起身來】

小：　（不標準的粵語）男人冇得話唔得！你教架！其實我都識講嘅，
　　　我係呢邊地住咗十幾年，已經係半個廣府人架喇！但係好硬

膠，我次次同啲人講廣東話，佢哋都掉番轉同我講普通話喔！
學俾你睇，我公司啲客。

【小波走近大波，雙手拍了拍大波的臉】

小：　（模仿廣東腔普通話）「你廢嗦（會說）普通髮，我也廢嗦，
　　　那為森摸不嗦普通髮捏？係不係？係不係？大家都意西意西，
　　　賊樣才有意西嘛！」草泥馬我就不懂了！你他媽普通話講得又
　　　沒我廣東話好，憑什麼接受不了我講廣東話！

【停頓】

小：　我他媽就是沒錢！誰有錢誰就是爺！我他媽要是李嘉誠的兒
　　　子，我要跟你說普通話，你敢說廣東話？！我他媽隨便抽一打
　　　錢都砸死你！對不對？你說呢你說呢？嗯？

【小波邊說邊用手輕輕摸了摸微波的頭，微波躲避】

【停頓】

小：　老大，得了這筆錢你想怎麼玩？

【小波去拔飛鏢】

小：　按我說，咱每人帶五個小姑娘……

【停頓】

小：　租條小船開去孤島……

【小波拔不出飛鏢，放棄】

小：　怎樣？！老大，咱快把合約簽了吧！

【停頓】

大：　好，飲完就簽。

微：　關於這合約，我還想跟你談談。

小： 你談。

微： 我簽。

【停頓】

小： 你簽？

微： 對。

【停頓】

微： 你不介意的吧？

小： 我無所謂的呀。

【大波從口袋掏出合約，翻到最後一頁放在茶几上】

大： 有冇筆？

微： 我去攞 –

小： 等等……

【停頓】

小： 微波，實話說，我有點不舒服。

大： ……

微： ……

小： 怎麼好像每次我都得按你喜歡的去做？

大： ……

微： ……

大： 一樣咁分啫，佢鍾意簽你咪俾佢 / 簽囉。

小：　老大，這不是誰簽的問題，憑什麼他想簽就簽，不想簽就不簽？

大：　（對微波）係囉，點解啫？下次唔好喇吓 —

小：　叫他給個理由我，叫他說，憑什麼 —

微：　我簽比較穩陣。

大：……

小：　穩陣？是說我不安全咯？

微：　（普）我沒說你不安全 —

小：　你就是這意思，你說，為什麼我不安全？

微：　（普）不說了，簽吧 —

小：　不說清楚誰都別想簽。

【小波拿起合約】

【停頓】

小：　我很怕你這一點，你就像個定時炸彈知不知道？！

微：　（普）不知道。

小：　別看你現在很平靜的樣子，真不知道你什麼時候「砰！」突然就爆了。每次都這樣，什麼預兆都沒有的！不信你問老大！

【大波聳了聳肩】

微：　（普）好我說，我覺得，我比你有信用。

小：　我不懂誒，我他媽做了十多年生意，什麼時候給你一種很沒信用的感覺？

大： 好喇好喇，做嘢講效率 –

小： 老大，我沒信用嗎？我沒嗎？

大： 點會啫，你生意人嚟架嘛。

小： 你看老大就比你明白。我到底哪裏得罪你了？你直接說！

微： （普）我……跟你……

小： 你說廣東話，你說。

微： 同你打交道我已經儘量直接架嘞，比如話前日，你對臭襪塞喺我鞋入面，仲有星期一，你又唔擦乾淨個馬桶，呢啲我都儘量第一時間話你聽／我唔滿意……

小： 很好啊，我就喜歡你這樣，我有生氣嗎？只要你願意 –

微： 我唔願意！次次我都要落好大決心先講到出口！

小： 那就是你的問題了，學着大氣一點。一點都不大氣，一點都不男人，那怎麼行？

【停頓】

微： 唎，就好似你投先嗰句「（普）一點都不大氣，一點都不男人」，就好可能令我成晚瞓唔着，然後慢慢演變為一種仇恨。

【小波電話響】

小： 喂，爸……還在談……再等等……我他媽也很煩你別老顧着自己好不好！！！

【小波掛斷電話】

【停頓】

小： （冷靜地）你看這樣，我們以後儘量不要說話。

微： ……

大： ……

小： 我們以後儘量不要有接觸，好吧？因為我不知道哪一句話 / 又會得罪你。

大： 喂，你講笑吖嘛！駛唔駛吖！

微： 你點得罪我都得，但係利用朋友就係唔得！

小： 又是利用，又是利用！我們早就吵過了是不是？我們也互相道歉了！你……不……你可不可以放過我？ / 我求你好不好？

微： 我放過你？呵真係搞嘢， / 好搞嘢。

小： 你現在就像你那本《不要控制我》書裏說的一樣，你在控制我。

微： 我覺得你控制我添，你連我點行路點講嘢着咩 style 嘅褲都要 judge。你自己唔曉，但你潛意識就係想控制我，然後充分咁利用我 –

小： 夠了！你有什麼好利用的？你不過是個小文員，又沒啥背景，現在又失業！我有什麼好利用你的？我在深港兩地打拼了這麼久，我能利用你什麼？

微： 知唔知你最恐怖嘅係咩？

小： 你說 –

微： 就係你連自己諗緊乜都唔知，根本控制唔到自己！

小： 那你說我在想什麼，說！

微： 你口口聲聲講咩理想理想，其實成個腦都係錢！女人！成個腦都 / 係成功！

小： 哎唷，王微波，我愈來愈搞不懂你，你就不想賺錢？！你就不想成功？！就你最有理想，你有很多很多的理想！別人都是屎！－

微： 我哋唔係同一個世界嘅人－

小： 微波，我知道你瞧不起我，我一直把你當親兄弟／但你一直都瞧不起我－

微： 唔好再兄弟兄弟，聽到就起雞皮！你根本就冇兄弟、冇朋友！唔信你問大佬！你問大佬係咪都咁覺？！

大： 你個腦係咪燒壞咗呀！－

小： （對微波）原來你一直這麼看我。

大： 你睬佢都硬膠嘅，我當你兄弟，我信你－

微： 你講大話！

【停頓】

微： 大佬點解你唔將同我講嘅嘢講番俾佢聽？

大： 講咩吖？有咩咁好講吖？

微： 唔係架，你唔係咁同我講架－

大： 都話冇嘢講囉，你硬係要逼我！

小： 你總是咄咄逼人知不知道？！／你很恐怖！

微： 大佬點解次次你都保持中立？！你就喺五張嘢喇講嘢仲係咁冇 point！

【沉默】

【小波一手按着合同，一手從口袋抽出筆】

【微波迅速按住合同】

微： 做咩 –

小： 你管我 –

微： 廢話 –

小： 放手。

【停頓】

小： 放不放?

【小波和微波爭搶合約，大波上前制止】

【酒瓶被碰倒，酒水灑了大波一身，合約忽地被撕成三份】

大： 好喇好喇好喇!

【大波邊說邊把兩人手中的碎紙奪過來，捏作一團，點燃後丟在煙灰缸內】

大： 大家都咪撚駛簽! 一個二個都唔好簽! （對微波）尤其係你! 你唔駛旨意攞到筆錢! 你覺得我講嘢無料到吖嘛? 宜家夠唔夠料吖? 駛唔駛俾多啲吖? 讀咁多書一撚啲用都冇! 係咪我五張嘢就要聽你哋吠? 係咪我五張嘢你哋就當我廢柴? !

微： ……

小： 算了老大 –

大： （對小波）唔好叫我老大你根本冇當過我係老大! 最貪心嗰個就係你。我承認，你有冂才! 有自信! 總之你叻撚晒! 但係你憑邊條撚講我冇用吖? 我駛撚你教我點做生意啊? 我駛撚你教我點做人吖? !

【一段長長的沉默】

【隱隱約約傳來工地打樁聲，牆上的鐘愈來愈不穩定】

【大波點了一支煙】

大：　你哋唔駛爭喇，份約其實都唔係咁易簽嘅。

【停頓】

大：　雖然個實驗唔係咁麻煩嘢，但係，合作期有成五年。

小：　……

微：　……

【停頓】

大：　五年之內，唔可以離境，唔可以缺席實驗，每次實驗前一個禮拜唔可以飲酒、唔可以食煙、唔可以搞嘢，如果唔係……扣錢。

【停頓】

【大波從口袋拿出一張新合同，捏在手裏】

大：　清楚喇嘛？

【一聲巨響從工地傳來】

【第二幕完】

第 三 幕

【公寓內，茶几上五份披薩疊在一起】

【隱隱傳來工地的打樁聲，牆上掛鐘的時間依舊不穩定】

【大波和微波】

【微波正將剪報往牆上貼】

微： 我第一次識佢係喺間髮廊，喺度洗完頭仲有人幫你揉骨。

大： 正……定邪？

微： 平時去親都係喺男仔，因我個背脊好硬，男仔手勁好啲，揉起
嚟爽好多。

【一女子上，開始為一名男子洗髮】

【打樁聲逐漸化為一股靈動的韻律】

微： 但嗰日淨係得女仔，我唯有將就下。Unbelievable，個女仔
手勢好好，perfect。佢抹咗啲精油喺對手，藕住我背脊，輕
輕輕輕咁慢慢攝入去，跟住，輕輕輕輕咁將我上半身微微抬高
半寸，對手好似兩條發光嘅鯉魚開始喺我背脊度遊嚟遊去，地
心吸力幫呢一對金光燦爛嘅鯉魚慢慢推散開我勞損嘅肌肉，嗰
一刻，我嘅生命彷彿得到咗解放，得到咗重生。我 feel 到，
一對非常勤勞嘅手，一對剛柔並濟嘅手，我 feel 到啲掌紋，
我好鍾意呢對手，我好鍾意好鍾意呢對手，呢對咁親切咁平凡
咁溫柔體貼嘅手。

【停頓】

微： 佢叫琳琳。

【同一地點】

【遠處打樁聲依舊有節奏地進行着，時鐘的指針依舊不穩定】

【大波和小波】

【小波在玩飛鏢。原來三支鏢仍然插在紅心中】

大： 你唔識佢?

小： 其實我一直覺得馬桶不適合中國國情。

大： ......

小： 全市人往上數三代誰家是用馬桶的?

大： ......

小： 五年。

大： ......

小： 也許我炒股發了,要回上海發展了 –

大： 即係你唔諗住簽?

小： 100 萬,我大概分得 25 萬,25 萬,五年,每年五萬,也就是每個月大概 4000 多一些。老大,你知道嗎? 最讓我頭痛的就是這個數字。

大： 咁你想點?

【小波將茶几上的五盒披薩分為左二右三】

小： 我讓半成,我二他三,讓他簽。

【同一地點】

【大波和微波】

【微波在剪報紙】

微： 我有陣時就想揸兩把刀仔,拍係枱面度同佢講: 「噂,呢度有把菜刀同把生果刀,你揀一把我揀一把,今日嘅事就喺度解決唔好俾佢出街。」

大：　你想劈撚死佢。

微：　咪住，兩把都係我買嘅，憑咩佢揀？！

【同一地點】

【大波和小波】

【小波在玩飛鏢。原來的三支鏢連同靶心都被摳掉】

小：　都二三分了，你是怎麼跟他說的？你怎麼一點用都沒有啊老
　　　大？（停頓）就這件事來說。

大：　總之唔係我等錢洗。

小：　我知道他瞧不起我。

大：　……

小：　他永遠是最好的最牛逼的別人都是屎。

大：　……

小：　咱上海人怎麼啦？全上海往上數三代誰家是上海的？

大：　……

小：　他本地人又怎麼啦？全市往上數三代誰他媽是本地的？！

大：　……

【小波將飛鏢靶掰作兩半】

小：　你就問他！假如他把我揍一頓就願意簽的話，來吧！我小波絕
　　　不還手！

【同一地點】

【大波和微波】

【微波在往牆上貼剪報，黑白一片】

微： 琳琳。

大： ……

微： 約過出嚟兩次，清純、善良，識唱歌添。

大： ……

微： 後尾唔知點解，傾下傾下我就變咗做佢姊妹嘞。

大： 嗱，細佬，老老實實，我個女失蹤成個月架嘞，我等錢洗。

微： 嗰晚個上海仔同我講，（普）「我好孤獨，好無助，不知道該怎麼辦。」

大： ……

微： 咁我替佢諗咗諗，不如介紹琳琳佢識啦。

大： 佢歡迎你揼柒佢，仲分你三成，真係咁都唔簽？

微： 你不如叫佢都替我諗諗？

【同一地點】

【大波與小波】

【小波從大波床上抽出一塊披薩】

小： 我很難過，我今天為什麼這麼難過？

【小波將披薩掛到牆上】

小： 咱把裏邊那馬桶砸了換個蹲的，怎樣？

【小波用披薩當靶玩起飛鏢】

大： 唉，你哋兩個好屎煩 –

小： 現在是他拒絕溝通。

大： 總之宜家唔係我等錢洗。

小： 我覺得揍他一頓就明白了，咱他媽要麼徹頭徹尾地做敵人，不要不清不楚，揍他一頓就明白了，真的。

大： 佢叫你諗都唔好諗。

小： 啥啥?

【大波將茶几上的五盒披薩分為左三右二】

大： 二三分。佢二，你三，份約你簽。

【小波將三支飛鏢奮力一扔，盡數飛出窗外】

【同一地點】

【大波與微波】

【微波在禪坐】

【打樁聲化為一股古怪而迷幻的韻律】

微： 咁嗰晚佢請我哋一齊食宵夜，我同琳琳嚟到見到枱面成抽酒。

【一名女子上，旁邊是小波，他們在喝酒】

微： 嗰晚小波好唔同，成個人變得好 charming，佢對眼好似識得發光，charm 到我諗男人都好冧佢。我哋玩猜枚，我第一個冧咗喺枱面。佢哋兩個飲得好開心，我好好奇，點解佢哋第一次就可以飲咁開心? 模糊之中，我覺得自己好似又返到髮廊揉緊骨，我見到有隻手喺條腰度來回遊走 –

大： 細佬，我……真係真係唔想無咗個女……再考唔到佢一定死俾我睇。

微：　咁埋完單，小波話送琳琳番屋企，我話一起。三個人蕩嚟蕩去，
　　　條路鬼影都冇隻，靜到似舊啫喱咁。我就近搵咗棵樹，冚唪爛
　　　嘔晒出嚟。等我嘔完擰轉面……

大：　……

微：　我一眼睄到小波攬到琳琳實一實喺度打緊茄輪。

【停頓】

微：　於是乎我繼續向前行，啲風愈嚟愈大，我一邊行一邊諗，我仲
　　　需唔需要陪佢送琳琳返屋企呢？

【大波將茶几的五盒披薩分為左一右四】

大：　四成！

微：　……

大：　細佬，我保證佢一個仙都攞唔撚到。四成，你簽唔簽？！

【窗外的打樁聲淡去】

【同一地點】

【大波、小波與微波】

【茶几上五盒披薩已經被從中間劈開，左右各半疊】

【微波一手按着合約，一手拿着筆懸在半空】

微：　（粵）它本是荒漠上離群索居的羔羊……

【停頓】

微：　又不是森林中玲瓏機智的灰狼……

【停頓】

微： 為何要它離開那片故土……

【停頓】

微： 來這深山裏找尋它的原鄉……

大： 實驗合約，分成合約，白紙黑字，清清楚楚，鳩噏多句都無謂，
簽咗再嗌最實際。

【微波把筆放下】

【停頓】

微： （對小波）我了解你宜家嘅處境……

【停頓】

微： 呢份約……

【停頓】

微： 我可以簽……

【停頓】

微： 錢，一人一半，你照攞……

【停頓】

微： 但係……

【停頓】

微： 請你先道歉。

【沉默】

【小波點煙】

小： 為什麼?

【沉默】

【微波拿出噴霧噴了噴】

微： （普）關於小琳的問題。

【停頓】

小： 小琳?

【停頓】

小： 什麼問題。

【停頓】

微： 你真係唔清楚?

【停頓】

小： 好吧，我很抱歉。

【停頓】

微： 抱歉啲咩?

【停頓】

微： 我想知，你抱歉啲咩?

【停頓】

小： 微波，我已經跟你道歉了。

大： 細佬，我有心臟病。

【停頓】

微： 我一定要清楚你抱歉啲咩。

【停頓】

小： 微波，請你弄清楚，現在不是我在求你辦事 –

微： 我要知你抱歉啲咩，我一定要知！仲有，請你唔好話抱歉，唔好用「抱」、「歉」呢兩個字！我要嘅唔係抱歉，請你講「對唔住」，「對唔住」！OK？！

小： 對唔住。

【停頓】

【小波電話響】

小： 喂，爸……還在談……沒鬥氣……嗯，一會兒說。

【停頓】

微： 對唔住啲咩？

【停頓】

小： 受夠了，我簽我簽！

大： 冷靜啲！（對微波）細佬，我哋之前傾掂晒架係咪？有咩問題簽咗份約先啦好冇？

【停頓】

大： 當俾個面大佬嘞，好冇？

【停頓】

大： （普）只要你願意……

【沉默】

微： 對唔住啲咩?

小： 好吧，微波，如果你覺得是我搶了你的女人，現在我很誠懇地跟你道歉，對不起。

微： ⋯⋯

小： 請你原諒我。

微： ⋯⋯

小： 你可以原諒我的。

微： ⋯⋯

小： 只要你願意，你相信。

【停頓】

微： Sorry 你話⋯⋯我嘅女人?

小： ⋯⋯

微： 我諗我哋之間有少少誤會。

【停頓】

微： 點解你認為你搶咗我嘅女人?

小： 你真的很恐怖。

微： 唔通一開始你就覺得琳琳係我女人?

小： ⋯⋯

微： 假如係，點解你仲要搶?

小： 我沒搶好吧? 你自己介紹給我的，我搶什麼喇?

微： 咁點解你話搶咗我女人？

小： 你不是這麼認為的嗎？你自己心裏不是這麼想的嗎？微波，我就是怕傷害你所以一直不想提這件事。

大： 講到尾都係為咗女人，簽咗份約我哋即刻落東莞！

微： （對小波）一，我有咁諗過。二，既然你覺得會傷害我，點解仲要做啲咁嘅嘢？

小： （粵）乜嘢？我做了什麼？

微： 你清楚咁話我聽，你同琳琳咩關係？

小： 就……朋友嘛。

微： 朋友。

【微波深深地吸了口氣】

微： 仆你個臭街……

【微波忽地跳過茶几撲向小波，被大波起身攔住】

【小波嚇得往後退，大波將微波往後拉】

【混亂中微波踢了小波一腳】

大： 冷靜！冷靜！

微： 仆你個臭街，你上咗琳琳，你上咗佢然後話我聽你哋係 friend！你居然話你哋係 friend！

【小波走上前】

大： 做咩？！撩交打啊？！行開啦！

【小波想趁亂踢微波一腳，卻踢在大波腰上】

大： 哎喲!

【大家都停了下來】

大： 哎! 哎呀哎呀!

【大波扶着腰，攀着一張凳子坐下】

【沉默】

【窗外的打樁聲逐漸清晰】

小： 你去問問小琳吧，為什麼你不去問小琳? 是的，我承認那晚我喝多了，但我問過你的，我問過你喜不喜歡她，我甚至送她回家前還問了你介不介意!

微： ……

小： 你敢說沒有嗎?!

微： ……

小： 你設的局，你說的不介意，你給我介紹的人，現在你又覺得我對不起你，你告訴我，我該怎麼辦? 我該怎麼辦?!

微： 我有講唔介意?

小： 是的! 我清清楚楚的問你，你他媽說了!

大： 有冇人可以攞支活絡油俾我?

【停頓】

微： 你咁開心，問咗一次又一次，我仲可以講咩? 我係話唔介意，但你有冇搞清楚我唔介意啲咩?

小： 還能有什麼? 那種情況下／還能有什麼?

微： 點解你唔問下自己先? 點解你一定要逼人哋同意你?!

【大波開始四周尋找活絡油】

小： 我說過有緣會考慮長期發展 –

微： Good，你搞完佢先話考慮考慮，掉頭又走去東莞玩女人 –

小： 你以為我很喜歡玩女人？你以為我很喜歡？如果不是因為無聊！空虛！我怎麼會想着去玩女人？如果不是這個狗日的社會他媽讓我根本養不起女人我怎麼會想着去玩女人？！！！

微： 之前個湖北嘅女仔呢？

小： 快分了！

【停頓】

小： 不，為什麼我要跟你交代這些？你有什麼資格審問我？

微： 因為琳琳係我嘅 friend –

小： 我沒有對不起她，你去問她，她也很喜歡我，你去問 –

微： 冇用架，佢已經俾你控制咗。

小： 你到底想說什麼？為什麼你不能相信我對她的感情？是不是只有你認為的感情才是真正的感情？我覺得你無藥可救啊知道嗎！

微： 「無藥可救啊知道嗎！」So much drama！你好假，由頭到尾都係假！

小： 為什麼你要這樣對我。

微： 你嘥我時間。

【停頓】

【窗外傳來更明顯的打樁聲】

微： 為咗你嘅咗我咁多心血 –

小： 別講得你好像很愛我 / 一樣。

微： 你冚嘭爛一晚搞禍晒! –

小： 你最偉大，全世界最偉大。

微： 你當我咩？馬夫呀？你嘅我時間嘅我感情，仲搞到我冇咗個最 friend 嘅 friend！

小： 這關我屎事？

微： 琳琳已經唔同我講嘢喇，以前佢望我嘅眼神一直都好專心 –

小： 你純粹是想多了 –

微： 想見她都難，我啲 SMS 一條都冇覆。我唔知你同佢講咗啲咩，佢又同我講咗啲咩。成個世界我就得佢一個 friend，得佢一個！你真係利用我到盡，好撚盡！好 — 撚 — 盡！

【微波呼吸紊亂，像哮喘發作一般】

小： 好吧好吧，我知道了……

【停頓】

小： 你嫉妒我。

【牆上的鐘跌落地上，隨即碎開】

【遠處的打樁聲進而化為強有力的節奏，似乎這間公寓瞬間就要崩塌】

【停頓】

【大波在微波的床底找到了一包用報紙包裹的東西】

【大波坐下，緩緩撕開報紙】

小： 說白了，你 ── 在 ── 嫉 ── 妒 ── 我。

微： ……

小： 我知道你很想揍我……

微： ……

小： 沒事，一會我們去外邊。

微： ……

小： 我可以再告訴你。

微： ……

小： 你說她是你最好的朋友？

微： ……

小： 知道你最好的朋友怎麼說你的嗎？

微： ……

小： 你以為她不知道你想上她？

【刮起大風，門被吹得噼啪作響】

微： ……

小： 你難道就不是男人？

【牆上的披薩和剪報掉了一地】

微： ……

小： 她說……

微： ……

小： 你是色狼。

微： ……

小： 有色心沒色膽的淫棍。

【強有力的打樁聲消失】

【「啪!」，大波從包裹抽出一把菜刀和一把水果刀重重地拍在茶几上】

【同時，三張床崩塌在地】

【停頓】

【接着，左右兩面牆倒塌在地】

【一片嘎然】

【大波拿起茶几上的一卷手紙，走進洗手間】

【長達半分鐘的沉默】

【洗手間內傳來兩聲巨響】

【洗手間門砰地被踹開】

【手紙被踢出了客廳】

【大波出來，手上抬着馬桶】

【大波慢慢走到茶几前，把馬桶重重一放，「啪」，合上馬桶蓋】

【中間那面牆也隨之崩塌，在黑暗的遠方出現了一個巨型馬桶，巍巍然如一座大廈】

【大波坐在馬桶上，點了一支煙，用力吸了一口】

【沉默】

【大波拿起一把菜刀，遞給微波，微波沒有反應】

【遞給小波，小波也沒反應】

【大波將兩把刀「砰」地砸在茶几上立住】

【大波慢慢起身，打開馬桶蓋，遠處的巨型馬桶亦然】

【大波將地上的書、抽紙筒、酒瓶、筆一一撿起，一邊說話一邊將手中的東西投遠地投進巨型馬桶，水花不斷濺出】

大：　（淡定地）其實，我有咩唔知吖。你估，我唔知你冇唸過還番啲錢俾我咩？ —— 你估，我冇懷疑過你係咪大學生咩？ —— 你估，我唔知你哋當正我憨鳩咩？ —— 你估，我唔知自己粗鄙咩？ —— 你估，我唔知宜家啲人其實鄙過我好撚多咩？一自從嚟咗呢個城市，我慢慢發現，冇知識冇文化都可以行走江湖，全憑兩個字 —— 兌鳩。宜家啲人唔駛同佢傾架嘞，你兌鳩佢就贏架嘞，仲可以慳番啲感情做人。呢個世界係得兩種人嘅啫，一種就係兌鳩人，一種就係憨鳩人。你哋，係乜鳩人？前排呢，晨早溜溜八點幾我嚀住五舊水揸咗兩個鐘電單車去到個咩婦產研究所嘅接待處，攞出份約同埋身份證俾一個後生仔，佢睇都未睇就問：「學位證呢？」我問咩學位證，佢話：「你憨鳩架？盲架？份約寫明話要學士學位證睇唔撚到架？」咁我即刻揸住部電單車飛返嚟鴻坑村菜市場攞個學位返到去經已係下晝一點，地面成 40 度高溫就嚟煎到我九成熟喇。呢次個後生仔又試望都冇望我就掟番張證俾我話：「喂，阿鄉你貴庚啊今年？睇撚清楚未吖？ 35 歲以下呀憨鳩仔！」咁我頂住出邊個火球飛返嚟鴻坑村街市攞番張 80 後身份證返到去經已下晝五點，我個屎忽熟晒架喇。個後生仔可能未瞓醒，佢望咗望張證，又望咗望我，話：「挑你老味堅憨鳩架？老人癡呆啊？！去精神科啦！」於是乎，我返到精……返到房，呆咗好撚耐好撚耐……一個電話嚇醒咗我！我問邊位，冇人應……「女！係咪阿女吖？玩乜失蹤呀你！你係咪好辛苦？辛苦就講！你唔讀冇人逼你架！唔好再考喇，咪考喇，我一賺到錢就送你出國！邊個話我個女唔重要？邊個講架？！呢個世界憨鳩唔緊要，你唔係憨鳩！全世界兜鳩你唔緊要，有我做憨鳩！你嘅世界有憨鳩唔緊要，我嚟做憨鳩！」，「吖先生唔好意思我哋興亞銀行高額貸款免息分期易借易還⋯⋯」

【茶几上小波的手機響起】

【大波將小波的手機投進巨型馬桶，接着將兩把刀也扔了進去】

【大波從桌上拿起那張卡片】

大：（普）「只要你願意，你相信。」

【大波將那張卡點燃，扔進茶几前的馬桶】

【燃起了三丈火焰】

【響起一陣沖水聲】

【全劇終】

ABOUT *BLAST*

In a city that is constantly being demolished and rebuilt, in an urban village so poor that its Gini coefficient is off the charts,
three lonely men with no house,
no car and no women squeeze into a bedsit with no past and no future.
From their debate of toilet philosophy begins an absurd and brilliant war in defence of the sperm.
The voice of the north clashes with the sound of the south; from ploys, tricks
and surprises comes tearful laughter.

The Heart Sutra (p.103) is translated by Harischandra Kaviratna, in "The Heart Sutra: Prajnaparamita-Hridaya-Sutra", *Sunrise* magazine, December 1996/January 1997 (Theosophical University Press).

The translator would like to thank Kevin Bartholomew, Richard Grossman and Zeng Yilin.

Characters

Wang Dabo, pizza deliveryman, 48
Wang Xiaobo, product salesman, 32
Wang Weibo, office clerk, 25

Note:
Dabo only speaks Cantonese but understands Mandarin.
Xiaobo only speaks Mandarin; his Cantonese is poor.
Weibo is fluent in both dialects.

* Contains very strong language used in everyday life.

The "/ " denotes the point where overlapping dialogue begins.

The "–" at the end of a line marks the point of interruption by another character.

Act One

Any rapidly developing Chinese city.

Hongkeng Village, or any urban village awaiting demolition and redevelopment.

Inside a rundown, rented flat.

A bathroom and a living room, that's all.

In the living room, against the three walls are three beds – **Xiaobo's** *(left),* **Dabo's** *(centre) and* **Weibo's** *(right). The beds on two sides are both behind a curtain. There is a small window in the centre wall; next to it is a dartboard with three darts. High on the wall is an extremely unreliable clock.*

A shabby old coffee table with two stools sits in the middle of the room. An ashtray, a cup and a roll of toilet paper are on the table.

Thunderous clamour from building sites comes through the window persistently. The minute hand of the clock drops a fraction with each thump of the pile driver.

Weibo *and* **Dabo.**

Dabo *is getting ready to go out. Weibo sits on the edge of a bed.*

Dabo   The landlord says when they're done piling over there, we'll be next.

Weibo   Hey, don't change the subject. I know how you feel.

Dabo   Feel what? I don't get / you.

Weibo   I mean, I know what it's like to fall –

Dabo   What? Fail what?

Weibo   No . . . fall, trip over. You're not young –

Dabo   So I'm ancient now?

Weibo   No, I mean . . . it's all right if things break –

Dabo   Break? Break what? What's broken?

Weibo   The bog.

Dabo   Oh, it's broken? –

Weibo   Yeah.

Dabo   Oh.

Weibo   The bog –

Dabo   Okay, okay, I've got pizzas to deliver.

Weibo   It's no big deal that it's broken –

Dabo   Okay! Wear and tear –

Weibo   No, it's not that –

Dabo   Then what? –

Weibo   I mean, can you not squat on the bog when you shit?

Powerful piling noise drowns out their exchange.

Xiaobo *enters. He looks out of the window with his hands to his eye as if he is looking through a telescope.*

A woman's silhouette appears on the frosted window across the street.

All sounds become indistinct. Time seems to have paused. Only her enchanting legs are moving.

She disappears.

Xiaobo *and* **Dabo.**

Xiaobo *is giving* **Dabo** *a massage.* **Dabo** *sighs contently.*

Dabo   Yes, yes, that's it!

Xiaobo   Here, if I press harder . . .

Dabo   Ah . . . ah . . . cracking . . .

Xiaobo   Have you read this book *I Love Money*, bro?

Dabo   Book? . . . ah . . . I can barely read . . . ooh . . . ah . . .

Xiaobo   *I Love Money.* It's Taiwanese, y'know?

Dabo   Ah . . . yes . . . cockload of milk tea shops . . . ah . . .

Xiaobo   "A well-off person may not know how to borrow money; someone who knows how to borrow may not be penniless. Some, through loans, successfully establish their network, the more they borrow, the richer they get."

Dabo   Ah . . .

Xiaobo   If a bloke always repays on time, who wouldn't trust him? Say, me. Would you not trust me, bro?

Dabo   . . . ah! Ah! Aah!

The Great Compassion Mantra music is heard.

Weibo *by himself, meditating.*

He recites the first few lines of the Heart Sutra up to "That which is voidness is bodily-form; that which is bodily-form is voidness." He repeats that particular line three times, pausing between each repetition.

The Great Compassion Mantra fades.

Xiaobo *appears on the side.*

Weibo *and* **Xiaobo**.

Xiaobo I always think I owe women a lot.

Weibo   That which is voidness is bodily-form; that which is bodily-form is voidness.

Xiaobo . . . you won't understand. How can you understand if you've never been in love?

Weibo . . .

Xiaobo Her body has a kind of purity. It makes me feel there's nowhere to hide my shame . . .

A plainly dressed woman nimbly walks out from behind the frosted window.

Xiaobo Her face, like a flower in full bloom; her laughter, clear as the silver bell. Like a glass of pristine spring water, you can't see anything, just exquisite – simple. Very simple. Very, very simple. So simple that you simply just want to lap it all up.

She disappears.

Xiaobo But we only see each other a few times each year. When I go to Hubei, all I can do is hang around while she and her father sell bananas . . . I feel really lonely and helpless, I don't know what I want to do.

Weibo   Have you been to the salon across the road?

Xiaobo   Salon?

Weibo   I know a girl there, she washes hair. I could introduce you.

Piling thumps make the clock hands move erratically.

In the flat.

Dabo *and* **Weibo**.

Weibo *is about to leave for work, he talks while he is getting ready.*

Weibo   Did you use the bathroom today?

Dabo   . . . yes.

Weibo   Did you take a dump?

Dabo   It's not me –

Weibo   Not you?

Dabo   It's really not me this time. When I got back from the pizza run, that's what I saw when I opened –

Weibo   I'm very particular about hygiene. I'll say sorry first, super sorry. I'm a pain –

Dabo   All right, all right, try to put up –

Weibo   Put up? . . . not with this . . .

Dabo   I really can't understand why we use a bowl in the bog –

Weibo   You know that it got on me! On my hands . . . and I haven't even had breakfast!

Weibo *exits, slamming the door.*

It is afternoon.

Dabo *and* **Xiaobo**.

Xiaobo *opens the bed curtain and comes into the room. He takes the toilet roll from the table and goes into the bathroom.*

Dabo   Remember to clean up.

Xiaobo *speaks from inside the bathroom, punctuated by heavier breathing that accompanies bowel movement.*

Xiaobo   When did I not clean up?

Dabo   Did you go this morning?

Xiaobo   Why are you asking?

Dabo   No reason. He asked me this morning why you didn't clean up after yourself.

Xiaobo   Asked you? Why didn't he ask me directly?

Dabo   Just asking. You weren't around. Did you?

Xiaobo   No. I don't shit in the morning.

Dabo *exits.*

Same location, evening. It is pitch black in the flat.

Weibo *walks in through the front door.*

Xiaobo's *voice booms unexpectedly.* **Weibo** *is visibly startled.*

Xiaobo In future if it's to do with me, ask me directly.

Weibo You off your rockers? Why didn't you turn the lights on?

Xiaobo *lights a cigarette. A tiny spark of light in complete darkness.*

Xiaobo Why did you ask him if I used the bog this morning?

Weibo *(in Mandarin)* I didn't.

Xiaobo You didn't?

Weibo *(in Mandarin)* I only asked him.

Xiaobo Did he?

Weibo *(in Mandarin)* No. Did you?

Xiaobo . . .

Piling noise ceases.

Midnight.

In the bathroom.

Dabo *on his own.*

Dabo *stares at the toilet bowl in front of him for about half a minute, his legs pressed tightly together. He takes a deep breath, pulls down his trousers and sits. Squeezing every last drop of energy from his body, to the point where his face flushes red, it simply is not happening. He stands up, lifts the seat and puts one foot on the bowl to test if it is sturdy.*

His lifts his leg and hesitates. He pulls some toilet paper to wipe the shoe mark off the rim. He then bends over to take his shoes off, getting ready to mount it barefoot. He hesitates again. He pulls lots more paper from the roll and lays it on the floor. Then he strides forward and squats, a move that looks very natural, very fluid and very assured. He feels immense pleasure from that instant he crouches down.

Xiaobo's *bed.*

Xiaobo *on his own, facing a beach babes poster.*

Xiaobo 'You've been waiting for a long time! Let us put our hands together to welcome our line manager, our hero and our mentor – Director Wang, Mr Wang Xiaobo!'
(Applauds then pauses.) "My dear fellows! How are you doing?"
'Great! Excellent! Fantastic! Yeah!'
"We must really, really love each other! Really, really love our friends! What do you say?"
'Great! Excellent! Fantastic! Yeah!'
(Gently.) "Then may I suggest, give the friend next to you the most heartfelt, heartfelt embrace. What do you say?"
'Great! Excellent! Fantastic! Yeah!'
(Embraces.) "Tonight, I will definitely help you find yourself! Find your direction! Find the meaning of life! Let us strive together, succeed together. What do you say?"

Weibo's *bed.*

The Great Compassion Mantra music is heard.

Weibo . . . Here, O Sariputra, bodily-form is voidness; verily, voidness is bodily-form. Apart from bodily-form there is no voidness; so apart from voidness there is no bodily-form. That which is voidness is bodily-form; that which is bodily-form is voidness . . . That which is voidness is bodily-form; that which is bodily-form is voidness . . . That which is voidness is bodily-form; that which is bodily-form is voidness . . . *(A single smack is heard.)* Here are two knives. One for you, one for me. What happened today, we'll sort it out here and now, within these walls!

Pause.

Weibo *takes a deep breath and resumes meditation.*

Music fades.

Loud construction noise comes in through the window.

Xiaobo *and* **Dabo**.

Xiaobo *holds up his mobile phone.*

Xiaobo You know why I didn't eat, didn't drink, didn't gamble, didn't whore to save five grand for an iPhone?

Dabo . . .

Xiaobo You . . . you know your biggest flaw?

Dabo . . .

Xiaobo Confidence. You've no confidence.

Dabo . . .

Xiaobo You know the one thing a man can't live without?

Dabo . . .

Xiaobo Confidence!

Dabo . . .

Xiaobo For example, your squatting broke the bog. Why do you have to squat? Why can't you sit on it? Why can't you accept new things from this metropolis? Because you've no confidence.

Dabo . . .

Xiaobo And look, these two buildings are worth 90 million but you can only rent! Please tell me how you are different from our landlord? Is he that many thousand times smarter than you? Is he? Is he?

Dabo No —

Xiaobo Then what's the difference? What?

Dabo Confidence —

Xiaobo Very good! Very good! Your confidence is starting to build slowly, bro. How do you build confidence?

Dabo . . .

Xiaobo First, you must see yourself as a neon sign!

Dabo . . .

Xiaobo In this day and age, if no one notices you, you've lost all your opportunities, you've fallen into the abyss! So? So? So?

Dabo Neon sign —

Xiaobo That's right! Neon sign! So . . . not having an iPhone means your values are skewed.

Dabo . . .

Xiaobo *(in Cantonese)* You know what a shake is?

Dabo . . . a shake?

Xiaobo *shakes the iPhone, the social media application WeChat makes a notification tone.*

He shows it to **Dabo.**

Xiaobo *(in Cantonese, calmly)* That's how you pull birds.

Pause.

Xiaobo So, an iPhone is not just an iPhone, it's also . . . also what?

Dabo A phone –

Xiaobo It's also life, confidence, esteem, status, taste, charm, aura, essence, everything!

Dabo . . .

Xiaobo A man can be penniless, but he must own an iPhone. Even if he can't smoke, can't drink, can't gamble, can't whore, he must bloody own the most dazzling iPhone – !

Xiaobo *exits.*

Dabo *goes over to* **Weibo**.

Dabo *and* **Weibo**.

Dabo If I've got a business.

Weibo *ignores him.*

Dabo If it can make a million.

Weibo *ignores him.*

Dabo   If I get you to join in the fun.

Weibo *still ignores him.*

Dabo   Oi . . . oi . . . whatcha reading?

Weibo   The paper.

Pause.

Dabo   What's in the paper?

Weibo   News.

Dabo   What's in the news?

Weibo   Headlines.

Dabo   What's in the headline?

Weibo   Someone jumping off a building.

Dabo   Somebody jumped? Why?

Weibo   To get in the paper.

Dabo   How?

Weibo   By jumping off a building.

Dabo   Did they have to?

Weibo   If it's not about someone jumping off a building, then no one'll read it. If no one reads it, then it's not news. If it's not news, then there's no point. If there's no point to life, then you may as well die. Since you'll die anyway, may as well die jumping off a building.

Dabo   Oh.

Weibo   So if there's a highrise, somebody'll jump. You think they're building them for people to live in? It's for people to jump!

Dabo   High . . .

Weibo   House –

Dabo   I know –

Weibo   Look, this schoolboy knew how to pick his spot.

Dabo   Even students jump?

Weibo   The whole world's doing their uni entry right now.

Dabo   Uni . . .

Weibo   University –

Dabo   I know. You've done it?

Weibo   'Course.

Dabo   Got in?

Pause.

Weibo   Mm.

Dabo   You got a degree when you finished?

Weibo   Mm.

Dabo   You got a cert with the degree?

Weibo   Mm.

Dabo   Can I have a look?

Weibo   8.30, time for work.

Weibo *walks out of the door.*

Piling sound drifts in faintly with a mystic and melancholic melody.

Dabo *on his own.*

A girl that looks like a student walks by in a distance.

Dabo   Daughter!

She stops.

Dabo   Daughter?

. . .

Dabo   Why did you run away?

. . .

Dabo   Did you fail to get in?

. . .

Dabo   It's not the end of the world.

. . .

Dabo   You've been trying for three years

. . .

Dabo   What more do you want?

. . .

Dabo   You want to go abroad?

. . .

Dabo   Is it really that great?

. . .

Dabo   You think I'm loser?

. . .

Dabo   You think I'm complete loser?

The girl exits.

Dabo   Hey! Hey!

Dabo *runs after her, exits.*

Xiaobo *walks in through the front door and slams it shut.*

Xiaobo *and* **Weibo**.

Xiaobo I don't understand, I exploited you? I only asked you to help move a few boxes tonight and I exploited you?

Weibo   *(in Mandarin)* I'm not talking about that.

Xiaobo What then? I've been away, I had no contact with you whatsoever, then I got a text saying I exploited you. I really can't work this out.

Weibo   *(in Mandarin)* Did you actually read what I sent?

Xiaobo What did you say? Other than saying I exploited you, what did you say?

Weibo *(in Mandarin)* I asked if you've ever seen me as your friend.

Xiaobo's *phone rings.*

Xiaobo Hey, Dad, call you back.

He hangs up.

Xiaobo 'Course you're my friend. I told everyone that you're my best bro, you can ask around.

Weibo *(in Mandarin)* I don't think you've got my meaning.

Xiaobo Please can you speak plainly then? Say it, what do you mean?

Weibo I . . . you can read this book, called . . . *Don't Manipulate Me*. It's quite good.

Xiaobo's *phone rings.*

He turns it off.

Xiaobo Weibo, let's not talk about books right now. Just say it, what do you mean?

Weibo I . . .

Xiaobo Say it!

Weibo I . . . actually . . .

Xiaobo You don't even know!

Weibo   Can you chill out a bit?

Pause.

Xiaobo Go on.

Pause.

Weibo   *(in Mandarin)* I . . . I think, you only see me as an investment.

Xiaobo What?

Weibo   I think you see friendship as an investment.

Xiaobo Investment?

Weibo   . . .

Xiaobo Yes, isn't that what friends are for? I be nice to you and you to me, both hoping to get something back in return? Yes, friends are an investment.

Weibo   What . . . what did you put in? Other than eating my food and using my things day in day out, what did you put in?

Xiaobo Oh, so in plain words you think I owe you and feel short-changed! My, my, I really can't work you out. I gave you money but you didn't want any. Now this! What do you want?

Weibo   We're all just trying to make ends meet. If I took your money, you'll probably swing the other way and say I'm no friend.

Xiaobo So now you're a friend? Pointing at my nose and accusing me, that's really friendly. It's you that's always saying we're brothers, best buddies and whatever, but all you've been doing is tallying up whether things tip your way.

Weibo I keep tabs on you? I lend you money and fix you up with girls, how am I keeping tabs?

Xiaobo Tsk, tsk, tsk, whatever, whatever. No need to be so blunt. You've just got your eyes on those few *kuai* of yours that I used and spent. I'll pay you back. Tell me. How much? Get it right. I'll pay half. Happy now?

Weibo Who do you think I am? Do I need your pittance?

Xiaobo Then I really don't know what you want. What are you trying to say?

Weibo You're never grateful.

Xiaobo What?

Weibo You . . . I . . . ah . . . I . . .

Xiaobo Wang Weibo, I'm telling you. I don't owe you anything!

Weibo . . .

Xiaobo Yes is yes. No is no. Stop faffing about! I'm telling you, I'm nothing like that. I'm not a scumbag who doesn't repay their loans. I'm not a scumbag who likes to take advantage of others. Is that clear? You know I'm about to crack from all the shit at work today? Now you're behaving like this and it just makes everything worse. Why is living with you more painful than dating? I'm shattered! I just want to cry right now! I really am shattered!

Silence.

Weibo Fine, I'll just ask you one question.

Xiaobo Go ahead.

Pause.

Weibo   Did you ever really see me as a friend?

Pause.

Xiaobo   You are my very, very, very best friend and brother.

Pause.

Weibo   Okay . . . okay.

Xiaobo *on his own.*

Xiaobo *(to his phone)* Dad, I owe a shitload in stocks too. Where do I find the money to lend you? No, Dad, I . . . What did I just say that puts the blame on you? . . . Dad, can't we talk properly? Why do we always have to argue? . . . Yeah, yeah, I shouldn't gamble. I should've given you all my money to trade! If you didn't lose all my money, how would I think of gambling to craw some back? . . . You . . I'm incompetent? Yes, I'm incompetent . . . I'm incompetent . . . My greatest incompetence is being your son! Being your son! You're always pulling my strings, pulling my strings, pulling my strings . . . constantly pulling my strings! I hate myself for . . . for being so like you! I thought, if I move out to try my luck, I could . . . shake you off. No-one will stick his nose in about who my friends are, what my goals are . . . but, I can't help it, I really can't help it. The longer I live the more I'm turning into you. My expressions, my temper . . . even how I speak! And your faults! All those faults of yours! And I can't even bloody stand those faults! A useless failure! You . . . you know, you ruin me. You ruin my life!

~ *End of Act One* ~

Act Two

In the flat, around eight in the evening.

Loud noise from building sites comes in through the window. The clock on the wall remains unreliable.

Dabo *on his own.*

There is a nine-inch pizza on the table. Half of it is already gone.

Next to it is **Dabo's** *mobile phone, an old Nokia with monochrome display. It vibrates for a long time.*

Dabo *takes the phone and slams it on the table. It stops vibrating.*

Xiaobo *enters looking exhausted.*

Xiaobo Hey.

Pause.

Xiaobo *notices the pizza and goes over to* **Dabo**.

Pause.

Dabo *pushes the pizza forward.*

Xiaobo Thanks, I'm starving.

They eat with their heads down.

Xiaobo You all right?

Silence.

Dabo *takes out a 12-inch pizza from under the table.*

Dabo   Finish this too.

Xiaobo   Forgot to wash my hands.

Xiaobo *goes into the bathroom.*

Dabo's *phone vibrates for a long, long time.*

Xiaobo *comes out with the book* Don't Manipulate Me.

Dabo *slams the phone on the table.*

The phone vibrates for the third time. He reaches out quickly and slams it down again.

He pulls out a thick stack of 12-inch pizzas from under the table.

Dabo   Help yourself.

Pause.

Dabo   You interested in getting people preggers?

Pause.

Dabo   There's money in it . . .

The phone vibrates.

Dabo *picks up.*

Dabo   Speak.

Pause.

Dabo   What?

Pause.

Dabo   My mate's eating.

Pause.

Dabo   Yes, my mate's eating your cheesy seafood pizza.

Pause.

Dabo   I know you don't want seafood, so I've asked my mate to fucking eat them all for you.

Pause.

Dabo   What, WeChat? I was already at the station when you called. What? We . . . WeChat your bollocks.

Pause.

Dabo   Yeah, yeah, yeah, you like WeChat, I WeChat your whole fucking family, bye bye!

Pause.

Dabo   What's WeChat?

Xiaobo *takes out his phone, gives it a shake. The social media application WeChat makes a sound.*

Pause.

Dabo   Go on.

Xiaobo . . .

Dabo   Finish them, my treat.

Xiaobo There's no seafood in this.

Dabo   This one you're eating, I got a call when I got to the station saying they want to switch to seafood cheese without cheese. When I got there again they said they wanted seafood cheese without seafood! I was on my bike for an hour!

Xiaobo *looks through the pizzas.*

Xiaobo Eh? Anti-radiation pizza?

Dabo   For the airport this one, the geezer's going to Japan.

Xiaobo Anti-brainwash pizza?

Dabo   *(in Mandarin)* "Sorry". This one's not for you, you're hopeless.

Xiaobo Each of these costs more than 200.

Dabo   Customers these days, if they aren't feeling fucking great they'll go: How can you have this kinda customer service in this day and age?

Xiaobo One, two, three, four . . .

Dabo   Fucking get Andy Lau to do this, stupid!

Xiaobo Ten boxes, that's like two grand. . .

Dabo   Nine hours a day, 40-plus outside, I'm riding all over town / for this bunch of cocks.

Xiaobo Actually, why is it called pizza?

Dabo   Then the missus in Zhanjiang called to say our daughter has disappeared for a month, / I just lost it.

Xiaobo Why isn't it flatbread?

Dabo   Disappeared for a month, the missus didn't say a word. I just blew up.

Xiaobo   What's the difference?

Dabo   I blew so hard, I even got a few . . . few . . . more piles. Then I still had to drive around town for nine hours. The bike fried my arse, cooked it through.

Pause.

Xiaobo *takes out a silver sun shield seat cover.*

Xiaobo   Here.

Dabo   Eh?

Xiaobo   Sun shield seat cover.

Pause.

Dabo   Thanks.

Pause.

Xiaobo   I may move.

Dabo   Move? Where?

Xiaobo   Don't know. I need a new job, or else I'll crack.

Dabo   People crack so easily these days.

Xiaobo   I really want to go back.

Dabo   Back to?

Xiaobo   Don't know.

Dabo   You fought tooth and nail to stay. Now you're going just like that?

Xiaobo   It's my problem. I've got problems –

Dabo   No, no. I'm asking why.

Xiaobo   I'm shattered. Every day I go out and see all these people on the street, I feel shattered –

Dabo   It's always that busy, just deal with it –

Xiaobo   I've been dealing with it for five years. I can't anymore –

Dabo   Why? Even I get by –

Xiaobo   I really can't. I can't –

Dabo   Why not? Real men don't say they can't!

Xiaobo   I don't want to. Don't want to! Okay?

Dabo   That's your problem.

Xiaobo   Yes, yes, I just told you. It's my problem!

Silence.

Xiaobo *shakes his phone. The social media application WeChat makes a sound.*

Dabo   You're skint?

Xiaobo *shakes his phone again. It makes a sound.*

He shakes his phone for the third time. It still makes a sound.

Dabo   You're skint?

Xiaobo Want to go to Dongguan?

Pause.

Dabo   You're skint?

Xiaobo Want to go to Dongguan?

Pause.

Dabo   You're skint?

Xiaobo Yes. I really want to go, but I'm skint.

Pause.

Dabo   You were born in '79?

Xiaobo *goes to play darts.*

Dabo   So you're 34.

Pause.

Dabo   Does your ID say '79?

Pause.

Dabo   What's your blood type?

Pause.

Dabo   Got STD?

Pause.

Dabo   AIDS?

Pause.

Dabo   I've got a contract, you . . .

Xiaobo   I really wanna go right now! Really, really want to go! I don't know why you just won't say if you're game!

Xiaobo *throws all three darts simultaneously. They fly out of the window.*

Pause.

Xiaobo   I haven't had a break for ages. I'll ask one last time, are you coming, bro?

Dabo   . . .

Xiaobo   That's how I look at it – don't know means no.

Dabo   . . .

Xiaobo   Don't worry about safety, I've got people there.

Dabo   . . .

Xiaobo   They're not like the birds across the road. Once you're there, you'll know what professional means.

Dabo   Pro . . .

Xiaobo   Skilled, skilled, ha?

Xiaobo *forms a telescope with his hands and looks across the road.*

A faint silhouette of a woman appears.

Xiaobo *(passionately)* Men since the beginning of time have been the masters of history, while women, since the beginning of time have been the masters of men. The ancients said, "A mind of steel melts at the curl of soft fingers." If you're an indecisive, suspicious man, go to Sichuan. The women are frank and fiery. Just like face-changing in Sichuan opera, their feelings and desires flow through words and expressions. What you see is what you get. No groping in the dark, no weary guessing. The purity of their personality will guide you on the right course, unless you are obstinate and opinionated. If so, you should taste Shanghainese women. You will find at long last you don't have to pretend to be a fierce lion, you can be a clueless, carefree Chihuahua. Their seasoned capability will give you a new lease of life and let you be reborn, unless you have abandoned yourself to debauchery. If so, you should go to Hunan. The women will make you realise that there is no end to self-abandonment. Don't ever try to peer into their heart. They may look like adorable little chillies but once you sink your teeth in, your tongue will get lashed. You'll understand the "inability to extricate oneself" really means "in pain, but euphoric". From them, you'll experience true sensitivity and the rare beauty that draws out compassion, unless you're blind. If you're really blind, if the light of your life has gone out and you're lost and confused, Dongguan will welcome you! Because there you don't need to pick and choose, you don't need to weigh the pros and cons, all you need is *renminbi*. In the whole of China, you won't find another place like this. Be it Sichuan, Shanghai, Hunan, etcetera, etcetera, etcetera, from north to south, from then 'til now, beauties from every region, skilled in hundreds of ways, all in the indescribability of Dongguan. The ancients said, "The smile of a backward glance brings a hundred charms; the beauties of six palaces gather in Dongguan." The ancients said, "The golden armour has seen hundreds of battles in the yellow desert, but there will be no retreat until Dongguan is reached." Whether in Taiwan, Hong Kong or the whole of Southeast Asia, Dongguan is the holy land where all men must make their pilgrimage! It takes no time to get to Dongguan, if you haven't been you're no real man.

Xiaobo *brandishes his iPhone.*

The woman disappears from view.

Dabo *catches the iPhone and studies it carefully.*

Xiaobo Here.

Dabo   110 km –

Xiaobo No need to look, I know it well.

Dabo   How long –

Xiaobo One hour to drive. We can get a cab.

Pause.

Dabo   Should we ask him?

Xiaobo What for?

Dabo   He's got a licence.

Xiaobo What good is that? He's got no car –

Dabo   I've got one.

Xiaobo Your bike?

Dabo   Four wheels.

Xiaobo Where did you find it?

Dabo   A friend just went home, his car's parked –

Xiaobo We can use that, we can. How big?

Dabo Huge –

Xiaobo What kind?

Dabo Pig's truck.

Xiaobo Any car's good. We can spend the night.

Dabo Easy. And save some money –

Xiaobo He'll come. He'll come for sure –

Dabo Yeah?

Xiaobo That one is a big lech.

Dabo Doesn't look like it –

Xiaobo You can't usually tell the big bad ones.

Dabo I thought he wouldn't like this sorta thing 'cause he's educated –

Xiaobo Don't you know? They're usually well educated . . .

Dabo . . .

Xiaobo Lemme show you something.

Xiaobo *goes to* **Weibo's** *bed and opens his bed curtain.*

Weibo's *bed is neat and tidy. The small bookshelf by the bed is stacked full of books. On the wall, a calligraphy work "Greatness comes from peace of mind" is hung. Around the calligraphy are cut-outs from newspapers and magazines. They are all famous paintings or artistic photographs. Over* *the headboard stretches a banner made out of toilet roll, with the words "Death upon your house if you peep again" written in large red print.*

Pause.

Xiaobo C'mon, let's have a look. Let's see what he's got on his wall. What's this? A man. A woman. Completely starkers. The man is on his knee sniffing the woman's . . . tsk, tsk, tsk, tsk, filthy! . . . What's this? Girls with big tits frolicking in the water with boys hung like donkeys! Tsk, tsk, tsk, tsk, so filthy! . . . What's this? Two she-males groping each other . . . too filthy! And this, and this . . . fuck me, fuck me. This is hardcore. This is not a woman . . . fuck me. Too, too filthy! Uber filthy! The funniest . . . funniest thing is . . . "greatness – comes – from – peace – of – mind"! Ah – ha – ha – ha! Have you seen anything like this? So damn peaceful, so damn great! Ha ha ha ha . . .

Xiaobo *is rolling on the floor, laughing.*

Weibo *enters, looking vacant. Three darts stick out of his backpack.*

Pause.

Dabo   Don't you have to work today?

Weibo   It stinks of fags in here.

Weibo *takes out an air freshener from his pocket and sprays.*

He walks past his bed then stops.

He puts down his backpack, closes his bed curtain and goes into the bathroom.

Xiaobo *pulls out the darts and puts them back on the board.*

Weibo *re-enters.*

Weibo Hey –

Dabo I didn't use it.

Pause.

Weibo Did you see the book I left in the bathroom?

Dabo Book?

Weibo Yeah, *Don't Manipulate Me.*

Xiaobo Is it this one?

Weibo *reaches for it.* **Xiaobo** *won't let go.*

Xiaobo Smile.

Weibo *grabs it.* **Xiaobo** *won't let go.*

Weibo Give it to me.

Xiaobo All right, all right. Look at you, so serious.

Throws it at **Weibo**.

Xiaobo Life's a mirror, boy.

Weibo . . .

Xiaobo If you smile, it'll smile back. Smile more.

Dabo Come, have some water.

Weibo *sits.*

Dabo　Back so early?

Xiaobo　You weren't fired, eh? Ha ha.

Pause.

Weibo　Yes, I was! Fired! Happy now?

Silence.

Weibo *on his own.*

Weibo　The office is usually dead when I get in. Today I saw a whole bunch of people all squeezed up by the door, said they were there for an interview. Before I sat down, the director called me into his room. He said, *(in Mandarin)* "You're still young. Even though your performance isn't great, I'll still give you a chance." I'm just a clerk pushing paper around all day. My only task is to lay out the company newsletter, make 30 copies and distribute them to the staff. It has the latest news of the company, speeches from the management. To make it prettier, I write a poem for the back cover. I asked if it was my poems that were bad. He shook his head and said I was a good poet. I asked him, as the internal newsletter is my only task, how do I get business out of the job? He said, "That's why your performance isn't great." I asked him, how do I get business out of the job? He said, "That's why your performance isn't great." I asked him, how do I get business out of the job? He said, "Then leave." I wanted to fucking pummel him, I raised my voice, "What's that chance you were talking about?" Then I picked up my pen and paper and walked into that dark and narrow corridor. His voice travelled out, "Whoever hands in the paper gets to be interviewed first." All of a sudden it seemed like there were tens of thousands of cockroaches flapping and flying on the wall. It didn't take long before it died down in the corridor, leaving me on my own. Then I felt someone pat me on the shoulder and say,

"It's dark, go home." I thought for half a minute, it felt like half an hour. Then I thought for another half an hour, what was I thinking just now?

In the flat.

Xiaobo You should've left pronto.

Weibo . . .

Xiaobo If you want to bollock him, then fucking bollock him. Why didn't you fucking do it?

Weibo . . .

Xiaobo You've all these education but you don't know how to fucking swear?

Pause.

Xiaobo Come, sit here. Sit in front of him. You turn around.

Dabo *sits with his back to* **Weibo.**

Xiaobo Imagine, this is your boss. Close your eyes, imagine . . .

Weibo . . .

Xiaobo Feel. The office, his face, his smell . . .

Weibo . . .

Xiaobo How long has he been there?

Weibo *(in Mandarin)* . . . two years.

Xiaobo Did he give you a pay rise?

Weibo *(in Mandarin)* . . . yes.

Xiaobo How much?

Weibo *(in Mandarin)* . . . 500.

Xiaobo 500 in two years. 250 a year.

Weibo . . .

Xiaobo You know *(in Cantonese)* how much those birds across the road make in an hour?

Weibo No.

Xiaobo *(in Cantonese)* Four ton. If you wanna press their bells, you'll have to save for two years, mate.

Weibo . . .

Xiaobo How did he treat you?

Weibo *(in Mandarin)* . . . nothing special.

Xiaobo No, he treated you worse than a dog.

Weibo . . .

Xiaobo Was he happy about your work?

Weibo *(in Mandarin)* No.

Xiaobo Why?

Weibo *(in Mandarin)* He didn't like me.

Xiaobo Why?

Weibo   *(in Mandarin)* I write poetry.

Weibo *reaches out with a piece of paper.* **Xiaobo** *takes it.*

Xiaobo *'Twas a lamb that left its flock on the heath,*
It was no agile grey wolf of the wood,
Why did it leave that familiar land,
For this mountain, to find its homeland?

Weibo   *(in Mandarin)* He thought I was showing off . . .

Xiaobo   He – is – jealous – of – you.

Weibo   . . .

Xiaobo   What did he say about your poem?

Weibo   *(in Mandarin)* He said, it's a pile of stinking dog shit.

Pause.

Xiaobo   A pile of . . .

Pause.

Weibo   *(in Mandarin)* Stinking dog shit.

Pause.

Xiaobo   Curse him with the dirtiest swear word you know.

Weibo   . . .

Xiaobo   C'mon, be brave.

Pause.

Weibo   *(in Mandarin)* You fuck.

Xiaobo Lame. Again.

Weibo . . .

Xiaobo C'mon.

Weibo . . .

Xiaobo After me – you cunt.

Weibo *(in Mandarin)* . . . you cunt.

Xiaobo Fuck your mother's stinking cunt.

Weibo *(in Mandarin)* Fuck your mother's stinking cunt.

Xiaobo Fuck your mother's stinking cunt, you son of a bitch.

Weibo *(in Mandarin)* Fuck your mother's stinking cunt, you son of a bitch.

Xiaobo Good! Louder!

Weibo *(in Mandarin)* Fuck your mother's stinking cunt, you son of a bitch.

Xiaobo Good! Good!

Weibo Fuck your mother's stinking cunt for churning you out, cuntface.

Xiaobo *(in Cantonese)* Perfect!

Weibo Fuck your fucking stupid, cock-sucking mother's itchy, warty, stinky, syphilitic, frigid, pox-ridden, clap-filled cunt. I've worked here for four fucking years, four fucking years, you cunt! I've had to look at your cunting face day in day out. It stinks more than my dog's arse! Whenever you see a woman you go lolling and yelping for attention, you fucking old fart. But when I asked for a tiny pay rise, you fucking hounded me to the ground. I fucking hope your shitty cuntface get smeared all over the pavement. I hope your stupid fucking projects get more and more fucking pointless! Think you're so fucking cool for employing all these fucking postgrads?! Think you're so fucking smart with your pig-witted interview questions?! Well, fuck you, you motherfucker. You never did a fucking day of work. You can suck dicks all your fucking life! Fuck your mother's cunt! Fuck your mother's stinking cunt! Fuck your mother's stinking cunt! Stinking cunt! Stinking cunt! Stinking cunt! Stinking cunt! Stinking cunt!

Weibo *wheezes as if he is about to have an asthma attack. He gradually calms down.*

Long silence.

Weibo   . . . sorry.

Dabo   . . .

Weibo *gulps down a couple mouthfuls of water.*

Weibo   . . . got a fag?

Dabo *gives him a cigarette.*

Xiaobo *lights it.*

Dabo *lights one for himself.*

Weibo *chokes on his first puff.*

Weibo *holds the second drag in his mouth, then exhales abruptly.*

He stubs out the cigarette in the ashtray. He then drinks a mouthful of water, gurgles and spits it into the ashtray.

Xiaobo Two years ago, when we first met in this tiny room, that night, I said something. Anyone still remember?

Pause.

Dabo Birds, anyone?

Pause.

Xiaobo I even gave you each a card.

Weibo Oh.

Xiaobo You remember?

Dabo Oh, that night we got loads of booze and went up to the roof.

Xiaobo You remember too?

Dabo Don't think you've paid for that yet . . .

Xiaobo I wrote what I said on the card.

Weibo I've still got it.

Xiaobo Where?

Weibo On my wall.

Xiaobo *dashes over to* **Weibo's** *bed, rips open the bed curtain, the words "Death upon your house if you peep again" blaze once more onto our retinas.*

He pulls the banner down.

He searches for the card on the wall.

Weibo *moves forward, tears the card off the wall and pulls the curtain shut.*

Weibo "Write your life in colour, have no fear . . ."

Xiaobo "Have no fear, because everything can be erased and you can start again. As long as you are willing, as long as you believe."

Silence.

Xiaobo Do you believe?

Silence.

Xiaobo To tell you the truth, I went gambling today. I lost all my savings from the past six months. But then it came back to me that I actually said this two years ago.

Silence.

Xiaobo And I said, I'll set up my own family business, *(in Cantonese)* I'll change this society.

Pause.

Xiaobo You said you'll become a great writer!

Weibo *(immediately)* No, I didn't.

Xiaobo You said something too!

Dabo What? Deliver less?

Xiaobo You said you want to give your daughter an education.

Dabo Yeah?

Xiaobo This is the time. Everything is starting afresh. Have you noticed?

Pause.

Xiaobo As long as you are willing, as long as you believe.

Pause.

Xiaobo Everything, is brand new. Like our landlord's house outside, and all the houses in and around this Hongkeng Village – demolish! Then rebuild!

All are visibly moved.

Dabo   Then you should really hear about this contract. It's proper freeloading . . .

Xiaobo Let's go on a bender tonight! / Let's plan our future!

Dabo   It's a medical experiment –

Weibo   Only a little –

Dabo   You can't not drink –

Xiaobo Let's go, to Dongguan!

Pause.

Dabo   Now?

Weibo   *(in Mandarin)* Dongguan?

Xiaobo Yes, Dongguan.

Weibo   *(in Mandarin)* To do what?

Xiaobo *(in Cantonese)* Do birds.

Pause.

Weibo *(in Mandarin)* You're going?

Xiaobo Yeah.

Pause.

Weibo *(in Mandarin)* You're . . . really going?

Xiaobo Yeah.

Pause.

Weibo Then go.

Xiaobo You're not coming?

Weibo It's not really me.

Dabo Hey, no rush. We can give you some time to think it over.

Xiaobo Feck, don't you think I didn't see how you grinned when I told you about Dongguan last month?

Weibo Yeah, I did when you talked about the sex workers. But it was / different.

Xiaobo A tart is a tart, what sex workers? Tell us, how is your grin different? What's so enchanting about it?

Weibo I've never said it's enchanting –

Xiaobo That's what you implied, even your grin is better than ours.

Dabo   If you've got any hang-ups, you can tell us –

Xiaobo You're so damn oppressed – why don't you run off and jump! Just don't jump too far and blame us when you die on the landlord's building site.

Weibo   I grinned, because I saw – sorrow.

Xiaobo Wot?

Weibo   I pity you.

Pause.

Dabo   Ha?

Xiaobo Pity? Who? The tarts?

Weibo   All of you.

Pause.

Dabo   Hey, I know you're a bit skint now that you've left you job. How about, I'll treat you if you come?

Pause.

Dabo   How's that?

Xiaobo . . .

Dabo   *(to* **Xiaobo***)* And you, too.

Silence.

Dabo   How's that?

Silence.

Xiaobo What are you cunts waiting for?

Dabo All right, we'll find someone else to drive.

Weibo Drive?

Dabo Borrowed a car. It's fine, I respect you.

Pause.

Weibo You can't find anyone to drive?

Dabo No.

Weibo Well, I can help.

Dabo You'll come?

Weibo I want some fresh air. To take my mind off things.

Xiaobo I know people there, no worries about safety.

Dabo So you're coming?

Weibo If you really can't find someone to drive . . .

Dabo We can't –

Weibo Then I'll come.

Pause.

Xiaobo Chop chop, grab your things. If we go now, we'll catch the first round!

Dabo I've got something to announce –

Xiaobo *digs under the table for something.*

146

Xiaobo Weibo, I cut some oranges the other day and left the knives there. Have you seen them?

Weibo . . . why?

Xiaobo Take them along, just in case.

Dabo I've got something to announce!

Pause.

Dabo It's good.

Pause.

Dabo If we sort it out tonight, it'll be all on me, as many times as you like.

Pause.

Xiaobo If we can't?

Dabo It'll be done. As long as you are willing, as long as you believe.

Xiaobo Tell us then.

Pause.

Dabo I've got a contract –

Xiaobo What is it?

Dabo Let me finish. On my way back the other day after a late night order, someone flagged me down, said they couldn't find a cab and wanted a lift. We got talking. It was a director of some medical research place. I did wonder what they were doing on their own this late – weren't they worried that I could be dangerous? . . . we got talking, and a hand moved south to my . . .

Weibo Director, she must be pretty old.

Dabo He.

Xiaobo Get to the point.

Dabo . . . I said, "How can I drive when your hand can't behave?" He went quiet.

Xiaobo The point, bro.

Dabo Then he said, *(in Mandarin)* "I'll give you a million. Spend the night with me." Whipped out his credit card . . . I thought, whoa, completely bonkers.

Xiaobo You're not asking us to be rent boys, right?

Dabo Could this be real? I couldn't make up my mind.

Xiaobo . . .

Dabo When I dropped him off, he gave me a card and said, *(in Mandarin)* "You're an honest man. Here's a contract, sign it and come to me at the research centre. It'll make you some money."

Silence.

Dabo That's what happened.

Pause.

Xiaobo The point! What you just said had no point at all!

Dabo They give you a million for signing up.

Silence.

Xiaobo *lights up and takes a drag.*

Weibo *takes out the air freshener and sprays.*

Xiaobo *goes to the window to smoke.*

Xiaobo Tell us about the contract. I won't sell my body.

Dabo Sperm donation.

Xiaobo . . .

Weibo . . .

Dabo I'm talking sperm donation.

Pause.

Dabo They're doing an experiment and need to make ten babies, five boys and five girls. So they need some geezer to give them his sperm. It's that simple.

Pause.

Weibo Then you get a million?

Dabo About the money, my thinking is . . .

Xiaobo Off to the bog.

Xiaobo *goes into the bathroom.*

Dabo . . . I found the deal, I want to be easier on myself and help you out, so whoever signs it gets 50.

Weibo 50?

Dabo   50.

Weibo   500 grand?

Dabo   500 grand.

Xiaobo *re-enters with a cup. He puts it on the table.*

Xiaobo   500 grand, deal.

Pause.

Weibo *leans forward and covers his nose.*

Weibo   You. . .

Xiaobo   Yeah.

Weibo   You use this to brush your teeth?

Dabo   Hey, Xiaobo . . .

Pause.

Dabo   The cup is fucking full of germs, they won't want it. Put your thing away.

Dabo *pushes the cup back to* **Xiaobo**.

Xiaobo *wipes the cup clean with tissues.*

Weibo   So, why don't you tell us about their requirement? See which of us is more suitable? How's that?

Xiaobo   Fine with me.

Pause.

Xiaobo But, I'm just saying, what if we're both about the same, then what?

Weibo He can decide.

Pause.

Xiaobo He may as well just decide now, eh?

Weibo That's not as fair.

Pause.

Xiaobo What do you say?

Dabo . . .

Weibo What are you afraid of?

Xiaobo Me? What have I got to fear? What about you?

Dabo Actually . . .

Pause.

Dabo You're both great . . .

Pause.

Dabo One is educated and principled . . .

Pause.

Dabo One is confident and good-looking . . .

Pause.

Dabo We're all good friends . . .

Pause.

Dabo   So . . .

Pause.

Dabo   I hope you two can . . .

Pause.

Dabo   Set down your prejudices . . .

Pause.

Dabo   And work this out . . .

Silence.

Xiaobo *(to* **Weibo***)* You first, what do you fear?

Dabo   Oi . . .

Weibo   What's there to fear? I'm not even scared of things that scare you.

Xiaobo   Fine. Please tell me, what do I fear?

Weibo   Don't you know?

Xiaobo   Ah, Weibo, have you got the balls to act like a man? You're just like a fucking girl.

Dabo   Oi . . .

Weibo   I warn you, show some manners –

Xiaobo   Okay, okay, sorry, my fault, I humbly apologise. Let's talk properly, eh?

Pause.

Weibo You said I'm scared. Why would I, a university graduate, be scared of you?

Pause.

Xiaobo Oh, he he . . . university graduate, so that's what scares me. Did you hear? University graduate!

Dabo . . . mm.

Xiaobo University graduate, how much do you earn a month?

Weibo None of your business.

Xiaobo A couple of grand? Where were you when I was making 20 grand in sales? Faffing around?

Weibo Move to a three-bedroom palace then, stupid!

Xiaobo *(in Cantonese)* Don't you know that three bedrooms ain't no palace? Virgin!

Dabo Okay, okay, okay. None of you get to fucking sign this, I'll sign it, all right?

Xiaobo I've always doubted if you actually went to university.

Silence.

Dabo . . . so . . . why don't you sign it?

Xiaobo Hey!

Dabo Split the 50 between yourselves. You sort it out. I don't have the fucking time to deal with you.

Dabo *moves away to play darts.*

Silence.

Xiaobo You or me?

Pause.

Weibo How're we splitting it?

Xiaobo Like this. One, two, three, four, five . . .

Xiaobo *takes five slices of pizza from the table and gives them to* **Dabo**.

Xiaobo Yours, 50.

Dabo *keeps playing darts.*

Then, **Xiaobo** *takes one slice and puts it in front of* **Weibo**.

Xiaobo 10–40 split.

Weibo 10–40.

Xiaobo Yeah?

Weibo Whoever signs get 40?

Xiaobo Yes, it's harder on him.

Weibo Can I sign?

Pause.

Xiaobo My Dad and I both owe a shitload in stocks . . .

Pause.

Xiaobo Altogether . . . 200 grand . . .

Pause.

Xiaobo I keep thinking someone's stalking me these days . . .

Pause.

Xiaobo I really hope you two won't get dragged into it . . .

Xiaobo *takes another slice of pizza and puts it in front of* **Weibo**. *Two on the left and three on the right.*

Xiaobo 20–30, how's that?

Pause.

Weibo My old man really needs money for his medical bills . . .

Pause.

Weibo But him and me know how to look after ourselves . . .

Pause.

Weibo I think you don't have to think too much . . .

Pause.

Weibo 20–30 . . . I'm okay with that . . .

Pause.

Xiaobo Then . . . deal? 20–30?

Weibo *takes a slice of pizza and puts it on his pile.*

Weibo Yeah.

Pause.

Xiaobo What's that about?

Weibo I'll sign.

Xiaobo *takes one slice back and puts it on his pile.*

Xiaobo Then you only get 20.

Weibo Why?

Pause.

Xiaobo *lights up the last cigarette, crushes the packet and throws it into the bin. He walks over to the window.*

Weibo *pulls out the air freshener and sprays.*

Xiaobo What should we do, bro?

Dabo Where have you got to?

Xiaobo Now, Weibo, let's not fight over this, let's split it in half –

Weibo Okay –

Xiaobo Half, each gets half –

Weibo Who'll sign?

Xiaobo Whoever wants to!

Weibo You then.

Pause.

Xiaobo Fine! No problem! I'll sign. I don't fanny around.

Pause.

Xiaobo Agreed?

Weibo Okay.

Xiaobo I'm popping out to get some fags then.

Dabo Sorted?

Xiaobo *exits. His voice travels in faintly from the stairwell, "Hey, Dad . . ."*

He becomes inaudible.

Weibo *takes the darts from* **Dabo**.

Pause.

Weibo You know?

Dabo Yeah.

Weibo I mean . . . you know, I don't despise him.

Dabo Yeah, yeah.

Weibo I know he takes the piss. Once or twice, I can handle that. Friends can't avoid that . . .

Dabo Fren . . .

Weibo Mates.

Dabo I know.

Weibo He's real smooth, really good at the surface stuff. Getting late night munches for you, buying you pants . . . he's given you some superman-print ones, right?

Dabo Yes.

Weibo I really appreciate the things he does to further our friendship . . .

Dabo Appre . . .

Weibo Thankful.

Dabo I know.

Wcibo But he'll never give anything away for free. He's probably been taking the piss all along without you realising. But I'm not stupid. I know full well every time!

Dabo And you still let him?

Weibo 'Cause I love him.

Dabo Ha?

Weibo Not . . . not that kinda . . .

Dabo . . .

Weibo I . . .

Dabo . . .

Weibo I mean, he is able to give me what I need . . .

Dabo Ha?

Weibo Not . . . not that . . . I mean . . . when I am lost, he can help me.

Dabo How?

Weibo Confidence.

Pause.

Dabo Oh.

Weibo I feel lonely and helpless all the time. I am a nice person with a not-so-nice temper. I really envy him sometimes. I want to be him. So direct. Never worry about how others feel . . .

Dabo No idea what you're on about.

Weibo It's all right. You don't need to.

Weibo *pulls the darts off the board.*

Weibo I mean, I've always seen him as a brother, but he just sees me as a dupe. If he asks, when did I ever refuse? If he needs money, when did I ever say no? And this is how he treats me? This is how he treats me? He . . . I really want to slam two knives on the table and tell him, you pick one, I'll have the other, we'll sort this out here and now, within these walls!

Weibo *stabs all three darts into the bullseye.*

Pause.

Dabo He borrowed from you?

Weibo Yeah.

Dabo How much?

Weibo A grand.

Dabo Paid it back yet?

Weibo No, it's not due. But he's usually on time . . .

Dabo He's also borrowed a grand off me.

Xiaobo *returns with two packets of cigarettes in one hand and a carrier bag full of beer in the other.*

Xiaobo Hey, fags for you, bro.

Weibo *(in Mandarin)* So much booze.

Xiaobo Fucl thc action, eh?

Dabo He he.

Xiaobo We aren't this jolly everyday, c'mon!

Weibo *(in Mandarin)* I don't want any.

Xiaobo *takes out a bottle of chrysanthemum tea.*

Xiaobo Ha, chrysanthemum tea, to cool you down!

Xiaobo *opens two bottles of beer, passes one to Dabo.*

Xiaobo I salute you.

Xiaobo *downs the whole bottle and opens another immediately.*

Weibo . . .

Dabo   . . .

Xiaobo You two are the only ones that I can truly call brothers. I salute you again, you're my real brothers now!

He downs the second bottle and pops open another.

Dabo   Can you handle it?

Xiaobo *straightens up.*

Xiaobo *(in awkward Cantonese)* Men can't say they can't! You taught me! Actually I can speak Cantonese, been here for ten odd years, half Canto already. But it's damn stupid, every time I speak Canto, they reply in Mandarin! I'll show you, those clients at my company.

*He walks over to **Dabo**, pats him on the face with two hands.*

Xiaobo *(tries to speak Mandarin with a Cantonese accent)* "You low Mandalin? I du tu. Den why dun we use Mandalin? Ya? Ya? We du it dugeder, dat's it!" That's where I don't get you mofo! Your fucking Mandarin is way shittier than my Canto. What makes you reject my Canto?

Pause.

Xiaobo It's 'cause I am fucking poor! Whoever's got money is king! If I'm Li Ka-shing's fucking son, and I want to speak in Mandarin, how do you dare answering back in Cantonese? I can just pull out a fucking wad of cash and slap you to death! Right? What d'ya think? What d'ya think? Huh?

Xiaobo *lightly pats **Weibo's** head while he rants. **Weibo** dodges.*

Pause.

Xiaobo What fun things are you planning to do with the money, bro?

He pulls out the darts.

Xiaobo I say, we should each get five girls . . .

Pause.

Xiaobo Hire a boat to a desert island . . .

He can't pull them out. Gives up.

Xiaobo How's that? Let's get it signed!

Pause.

Dabo Sure, after the drinks.

Weibo About the contract, I'd still like to talk to you.

Xiaobo Speak.

Weibo I'll sign.

Pause.

Xiaobo You'll sign?

Weibo Yes.

Pause.

Weibo You don't mind?

Xiaobo 'Course not.

Dabo *pulls out the contract from his pocket, turns to the last page and puts it on the table.*

Dabo   Pen?

Weibo   I'll get it –

Xiaobo   Hang on . . .

Pause.

Xiaobo   Weibo, frankly, I'm not too comfortable with this.

Dabo   . . .

Weibo   . . .

Xiaobo   How come I've to bend to your liking every time?

Dabo   . . .

Weibo   . . .

Dabo   You get as much anyway. If that's what he wants, let him / sign it.

Xiaobo   It's not who signs it. What's he got that lets him sign, or not, just like that?

Dabo   *(to* **Weibo***)* Yeah, why? Don't do that again –

Xiaobo   Tell him to give me a reason, tell us, why –

Weibo   It'll be more reliable.

Dabo   . . .

Xiaobo   Reliable? Are you saying I'm not sound?

Weibo   *(in Mandarin)* I'm not saying that –

Xiaobo That's what you meant. Tell us, why am I not sound?

Weibo *(in Mandarin)* Nah, let's just sign this –

Xiaobo No one signs until we're clear.

Xiaobo *picks up the contract.*

Pause.

Xiaobo This side of you really bothers me. You're like a ticking bomb, you know?

Weibo *(in Mandarin)* No.

Xiaobo You may look all peace and calm now, but no one really knows when you'll suddenly go "boom". You're always like that. No warning whatsoever. Ask him if you don't believe me.

Dabo *shrugs.*

Weibo *(in Mandarin)* Fine, I'll tell you. I think I'm more trustworthy.

Xiaobo I don't get it. I've been doing business for ten fucking years. When did I seem untrustworthy to you?

Dabo Okay, okay, can we just hurry up –

Xiaobo Am I not trustworthy? Am I not?

Dabo How can that be? You're a man of business.

Xiaobo See, he's more clear-headed. How did I piss you off? Just say it!

Weibo *(in Mandarin)* Me . . . and you . . .

Xiaobo Speak Cantonese, say it.

Weibo I try to be more direct when I'm dealing with you. Say the other day, you stuffed your smelly socks into my shoes. And on Monday, you didn't clean up after using the toilet. Things like that I tried to tell you as soon as possible that / I'm not happy . . .

Xiaobo Very good, I like you like this. Am I angry? As long as you're willing –

Weibo I'm not! I really need to screw up my resolve every time before I can bring it up.

Xiaobo Then that's your problem. Be less petty. You're so petty, not like a man at all. That ain't gonna work.

Pause.

Weibo See, like what you just said, *(in Mandarin)* "You're so petty, not like a man at all." Could well keep me awake all night. Slowly that grows into hatred.

Xiaobo's *phone rings.*

Xiaobo Hey, Dad . . . still talking . . . wait a mo . . . I'm fucking annoyed too, so stop just thinking about yourself!

He hangs up.

Pause.

Xiaobo *(calmly)* How about we avoid talking to each other?

Weibo . . .

Dabo . . .

Xiaobo We'll avoid any contact too, how's that? Because I don't know when I'll say something that / pisses you off again.

Dabo Oi, joking, right? That's a bit much!

Pause.

Weibo You can piss me off, but you can't exploit friends!

Xiaobo Exploit again, exploit! Haven't we argued over that already? We've both apologised! You . . . no . . . can't you just let me be? / I beg you, all right?

Weibo Let you be? Ha, that's rich, / that's really rich.

Xiaobo You're just like that book of yours *Don't Manipulate Me.* You're manipulating me –

Weibo I think you're manipulating me. You even judge how I walk, how I talk, what sort of trousers I wear. You probably don't realise, but your subconscious wants to manipulate me and then fully exploit me –

Xiaobo Enough! What's there to exploit? You're just a clerk, you've got no connections. Now you've lost your job! What's in it for me? I've been roaming Shenzhen and Hong Kong for years, what can I use you for?

Weibo You know what the nastiest thing is about you?

Xiaobo Tell me –

Weibo You don't even know what you're thinking. You can't even control yourself!

Xiaobo Then tell me. Say it!

Weibo Aspirations are always on your lips, but your head is just full of money! Women! Your head is all / about success!

Xiaobo Ah, Wang Weibo, I really understand you less and less. Don't you want to make money? Don't you want to make it? Only you're allowed aspirations, you're full of them! Everyone else is shit! –

Weibo We're from different worlds –

Xiaobo Weibo, I know you despise me. I've always seen you as my bro / but you've always looked down on me –

Weibo Can you stop the whole bro thing, it makes me cringe! You never had any brothers, any friends. If you don't believe me, ask him. Ask him if he feels the same!

Dabo Are you out of your mind? –

Xiaobo *(to **Weibo**)* That's who I am to you.

Dabo You'd be damn stupid to listen to him. I see you as a brother, I trust you –

Weibo You lie!

Pause.

Weibo Why don't you tell him what you've told me?

Dabo What? What's there to say?

Weibo No, that's not what you told me –

Dabo I said there's nothing to say, why are you pushing me?

Xiaobo You know you're always such a bully. / You're a nasty piece of work!

Weibo Why do you always stay neutral? You're almost 50, why don't you ever take a stand?

Silence.

Xiaobo *presses one hand on the contract and pulls out a pen with the other.*

Weibo *quickly slaps his hand onto the contract.*

Weibo What –

Xiaobo None of your –

Weibo Bollocks –

Xiaobo Let go.

Pause.

Xiaobo Will you let go?

Xiaobo *and* **Weibo** *fight over the contract.* **Dabo** *steps in to stop them.*

The beer bottles topple, spilling all over **Dabo**. *In a blink, the contract is torn into three.*

Dabo All right, all right, all right!

Dabo *snatches whatever is left of the contract from the other two as he speaks. He crushes it into a ball, sets it ablaze and drops it into the ashtray.*

Dabo No one fucking signs anything! None of you gets to sign it! *(to* **Weibo***)* Especially you! Don't even think about getting the money! You think I talk with no balls, eh? Is this balls enough now? Do you want more? All that education and you're still a fucking twit! Is it 'cause I'm 50 I've to listen to your yelps? Is it 'cause I'm 50 you all think I'm a duffer?

Weibo . . .

Xiaobo Let it go, bro –

Dabo *(to* **Xiaobo***)* Don't call me bro, you've never seen me as a brother! You're the greediest here! I admit that you've got a silver tongue. You've got confidence. You're the most fucking amazing! But who the fuck are you to say that I'm a twit? Do I need you to fucking teach me how to do business? Do I need you to fucking teach me how to live?

A long, long silence.

Piling noise drifts in faintly. The clock on the wall becomes more and more unreliable.

Dabo *lights up.*

Dabo You don't have to fight, it's not that simple.

Pause.

Dabo The experiment isn't much, but it lasts for five years.

Xiaobo . . .

Weibo . . .

Pause.

Dabo For five years, you can't leave the country, you can't miss a session. For a week before each session, you can't drink, you can't smoke, you can't shag, or else they . . . knock off the total.

Pause.

He takes out a new contract from his pocket, gripping it in his hand.

Dabo All clear?

A loud bang from a building site.

~ End of Act Two ~

Act Three

In the flat. Five pizza boxes are stacked on the coffee table.

Piling noise drifts through the window faintly. The clock on the wall is still unreliable.

Dabo *and* **Weibo**.

Weibo *is sticking newspaper cut-outs onto the wall.*

Weibo   The first time I met her was at the salon. They give you a massage after washing your hair.

Dabo   Standard . . . or happy?

Weibo   I usually ask for a man. My back is always really stiff. Men have more strength, it feels better.

A woman enters. She starts washing a man's hair.

Piling noise gradually morphs into a spirited rhythm.

Weibo   That day, they only had girls left, so I had no choice. Unbelievable. That girl really knew what she was doing. It was perfect. Her hands covered in essence oil, glued to my back. Gently she let the oil slowly absorb. Then, gently she lifted my torso up a fraction. Her hands, like two glistening carps, glided up and down my back. Gravity propelled them to gradually dispel the tiredness in my muscles. At that moment, my life seemed to be liberated, revived. I could feel those hardworking hands, those hands that contained both strength and gentleness. I could feel the prints of her palm. I really liked those hands. I really, really liked those hands, those kindly, ordinary, gentle, caring hands.

Pause.

Weibo   Her name is Linlin.

Same location.

Piling noise from a distance continues to beat away rhythmically. The hands of the clock remain unsteady.

Dabo *and* **Xiaobo**.

Xiaobo *is playing darts. Three darts are still sticking out of the bullseye.*

Dabo   You don't know her?

Xiaobo   I've always thought the bog doesn't suit the state of the Chinese nation.

Dabo   . . .

Xiaobo   How many people in this town have used the bog for more than three generations?

Dabo   . . .

Xiaobo   Five years.

Dabo   . . .

Xiaobo   Maybe I'll hit jackpot in stocks, head back to Shanghai to develop –

Dabo   You're not signing?

Xiaobo   A million, I get 250 grand. Five years, so 50 grand a year. That's about four grand a month. Y'know what? That number really hurts my head.

Dabo   What do you want?

Xiaobo *splits the pizzas into two stacks, two on the left, three on the right.*

Xiaobo I'll give him another five per cent, I get 20, him 30. He signs.

Same location.

Dabo *and* **Weibo**.

Weibo *is cutting newspaper.*

Weibo Sometimes I really want to slam two knives on the table and say to him, "Hey, here's a vegetable knife and a fruit knife, you pick one, I'll have the other, we'll sort this out here and now, within these walls!

Dabo You want to fucking hack him to death?

Weibo Hang on, I paid for both knives. Why does he get to choose?

Same location.

Dabo *and* **Xiaobo**.

Xiaobo *is playing darts. The bullseye is ripped out of the board together with the three darts that were stuck on it.*

Xiaobo Splitting 20–30 already. How did you talk to him? How could you be so useless? *(Pause.)* In this.

Dabo It's not me who needs the money.

Xiaobo I know he despises me.

Dabo . . .

Xiaobo He's always the best, the most fan-bloody-tastic. Everyone else is shit.

Dabo . . .

Xiaobo What's so great about us Shanghainese? How many of us can say we are from Shanghai going back three generations?

Dabo . . .

Xiaobo What's so great about him being local? How many people can say they're from 'round here going back three generations?

Dabo . . .

Xiaobo *snaps a dart into two.*

Xiaobo Ask him this! I'll let him punch me if that'll make him sign. C'mon! I won't lift a finger!

Same location.

Dabo *and* **Weibo**.

Weibo *is sticking newspaper cut-outs onto the wall, turning it black and white.*

Weibo Linlin.

Dabo . . .

Weibo We went out a couple of times. Pure, kind, a good singer.

Dabo . . .

Weibo Then I don't know what happened. We talked and talked and I became a girl friend.

Dabo   Hey, honestly, my daughter has been missing for a month now. I need the money.

Weibo   That night, that Shanghai boy told me, *(in Mandarin)* "I'm really lonely, really helpless, I don't know what to do."

Dabo   . . .

Weibo   Then I thought it over from his standpoint. Why not introduce him to Linlin?

Dabo   He asks you to beat the shit out of him. And he gives you 30. You really won't sign?

Weibo   Why don't you ask him to think it over from my standpoint?

Same location.

Dabo *and* **Xiaobo**.

Xiaobo *pulls out a pizza from* **Dabo's** *bed.*

Xiaobo I feel wretched. Why do I feel so wretched today?

He puts the pizza up on the wall.

Xiaobo Let's smash the bog and get a squat one, what d'ya think?

He uses the pizza as a dartboard.

Dabo   Argh, you two are such annoying cunts –

Xiaobo It's him who refuses to talk.

Dabo   It's not me who needs the money.

Xiaobo He needs a few punches to knock some sense into him. Why do we have to be fucking enemies through and through? Why can't we just muddle along? He needs some sense kicked into him, really.

Dabo He said don't even dream about it.

Xiaobo Wot?

Xiaobo *splits the pizza boxes on the table into two stacks, three on the left and two on the right.*

Dabo 20–30 split. You 30, him 20. You sign.

Xiaobo *throws all three darts hard. They all fly out of the window.*

Same location.

Dabo *and* **Weibo***.*

Weibo *is meditating.*

The piling noise turns into an odd, psychedelic rhythm.

Weibo That night, he bought us a late night chow. When Linlin and I got there, we saw a table full of booze.

A woman enters. On her side is **Xiaobo***. They are drinking.*

Weibo That night, Xiaobo was another person. His whole person became really charming. His eyes seemed to glow. He was so charming that even men would fall for him. We played drinking games. I was the first to get trolleyed. The two of them were having so much fun. I was really, really curious. How come they were having that much fun when they had only just met? In a drunken haze, I felt I was back in the salon getting a message. I saw a hand gliding around her waist –

Dabo   I . . . really, really don't want to lose my daughter . . . if she fails again, she'll kill herself for sure.

Weibo   We got the bill. Xiaobo said he wanted to walk Linlin home. I said I'd come along. The three of us stumbled around. The street was utterly deserted, not a soul in sight, the quietness thick as jelly. I found a tree to lean on and threw absolutely everything back up. When I turned around, I . . .

Dabo   . . .

Weibo   I caught a glimpse of Xiaobo clutching Linlin real tight and snogging hard.

Pause.

Weibo   So I kept walking forward. The wind got up. I kept thinking, did I still need to see Linlin home with him?

Dabo *splits the pizza boxes on the table into one pile of four and a single box.*

Dabo   40 per cent!

Weibo   . . .

Dabo   I promise you he won't get his filthy mitts on one fucking penny of this. 40, would you sign?

Piling noise fades.

Same location.

Dabo, **Xiaobo** *and* **Weibo**.

The pizza boxes on the table have been cut down the middle, with half the pile on each side.

Weibo *presses one hand onto the contract, his other hand hovering mid-air holding a pen.*

Weibo *(in Cantonese)* 'Twas a lamb that left its flock on the heath . . .

Pause.

Weibo *It was no agile grey wolf of the wood . . .*

Pause.

Weibo *Why did it leave that familiar land . . .*

Pause.

Weibo *For this mountain, to find its homeland . . .*

Dabo Contract for the experiment. Contract for splitting money. Clearly written in black and white. It doesn't matter if you've got anything else to fucking moan about. Sign it first then talk.

Weibo *puts the pen down.*

Pause.

Weibo *(to* **Xiaobo***)* I understand your situation right now . . .

Pause.

Weibo The contract . . .

Pause.

Weibo I can sign . . .

Pause.

Weibo   The money, we'll split it equally. You can take your portion . . .

Pause.

Weibo   But . . .

Pause.

Weibo   Please apologise first.

Silence.

Xiaobo *lights a cigarette.*

Xiaobo   Why?

Silence.

Weibo *takes out the air freshener and sprays.*

Weibo   *(in Mandarin)* About Xiaolin.

Pause.

Xiaobo   Xiaolin?

Pause.

Xiaobo   What about her?

Pause.

Weibo   You really have no idea?

Pause.

Xiaobo   Fine, I apologise.

Pause.

Weibo   What for?

Pause.

Weibo   I want to know, what you are apologising for?

Pause.

Xiaobo   Weibo, I've already apologised.

Dabo   Hey, my heart is weak.

Pause.

Weibo   I need to be certain why you're apologising.

Pause.

Xiaobo   Weibo, get this straight. I'm not begging you to do this –

Weibo   I must know why you're apologising, I must! And, please don't just "apologise", not that word! I don't just want an apology. Can't you say "sorry"? "Sorry"! Okay?

Xiaobo   Sorry.

Pause.

Xiaobo's *phone rings.*

Xiaobo   Hey, Dad . . . still talking . . . no rows . . . mm, talk in a bit.

Pause.

Weibo   What are you sorry for?

Pause.

Xiaobo   I've had enough! I'll sign, I'll sign.

Dabo   Calm down! *(To* **Weibo***)* Hey, didn't we sort this all out? Whatever hang-ups you've got, just sign first, eh?

Pause.

Dabo   For me, eh?

Pause.

Dabo   *(in Mandarin)* As long as you are willing . . .

Silence.

Weibo   What are you sorry for?

Xiaobo   Fine, Weibo. If you think I've snatched your bird, then I sincerely apologise. Sorry.

Weibo   . . .

Xiaobo   Please forgive me.

Weibo   . . .

Xiaobo   You can forgive me.

Weibo   . . .

Xiaobo   As long as you are willing, as long as you believe.

Pause.

Weibo   Sorry, did you say . . . my bird?

Xiaobo . . .

Weibo I think we've got a bit of a misunderstanding going on here.

Pause.

Weibo Why did you think you've taken my girl?

Xiaobo You're a nasty piece of work.

Weibo Unless you thought Linlin was mine from the start?

Xiaobo . . .

Weibo If so, why did you still take her from me?

Xiaobo I didn't, all right? You introduced her to me, what did I take?

Weibo Then why did you say you took my girl?

Xiaobo Isn't that what you want? Isn't that what you're thinking deep down? Weibo, I don't want to hurt you, that's why I didn't want to bring it up.

Dabo So, it's really just about women. Let's get this signed and we'll go straight to Dongguan.

Weibo *(to **Xiaobo**)* First, it never occurred to me. Second, if you knew it would hurt me, why did you still do it?

Xiaobo *(in Cantonese)* What? What did I do?

Weibo Tell me plainly, what's your relationship with Linlin?

Xiaobo Well . . . friends.

Weibo   Friends.

Weibo *takes a deep breath.*

Weibo   Fuck off and die . . .

Weibo *leaps across the table toward* **Xiaobo**. **Dabo** *stands up to stop him.*

Xiaobo *backs up in fright. Dabo tries to pull* **Weibo** *back.*

In the tussle, **Weibo** *kicks* **Xiaobo**.

Dabo   Calm down! Calm down!

Weibo   Fuck off and die. You shagged Linlin. You shagged her then you tell me you're friends. You actually call yourselves friends!

Xiaobo *moves forward.*

Dabo   What're you doing? Starting a fight, ha? Back off!

Xiaobo *tries to kick* **Weibo** *in the commotion, but the kick lands on* **Dabo's** *midriff.*

Dabo   Ow!

Everyone stops.

Dabo   Ow! Ow, ow!

Dabo *hunches over, grabs a chair and lowers himself.*

Silence.

Piling noise outside becomes more distinct.

Xiaobo Just ask Xiaolin. Why don't you ask Xiaolin? Yes, I admit that I drank too much that night. But I did ask you. I asked you if you liked her. I even asked you before I walked her home if you'd mind.

Weibo . . .

Xiaobo Can you deny that?

Weibo . . .

Xiaobo You set this all up. You said you didn't mind. You introduced me to her. Now you think I've done you wrong. Tell me, what should I have done? What should I have done?

Weibo Did I say I didn't mind?

Xiaobo Yes. I asked you outright, you fucking answered.

Dabo Can someone bring me some ointment?

Pause.

Weibo You were so happy. You asked again and again. What could I say? I said I don't mind, but did you work out what I meant – what I didn't mind?

Xiaobo What else? At that time / what else could it be?

Weibo Why don't you ask yourself first? Why do you have to force others to agree with you?

Dabo *goes around the room in search of an ointment to soothe the kick.*

Xiaobo I told her if this is meant to be, we can consider developing this long –

Weibo Good. You shagged her then you said you'll think about it. You turned 'round and went to Dongguan –

Xiaobo You think I really like tarts? You think I really like them? If it wasn't for boredom, emptiness! You think I'd go to them? If it's not for this dogshit world where I can't afford to keep my own fucking woman, you think I would need to go to them?

Weibo What about that Hubei girl?

Xiaobo Almost over!

Pause.

Xiaobo No. Why do I have to explain all this? What gives you the right to interrogate me?

Weibo Because Linlin is my friend –

Xiaobo I did her no wrong. Ask her yourself. She really likes me. Ask –

Weibo There's no point. She's already under your manipulation.

Xiaobo What are you trying to say? Why can't you believe my feelings towards her? Is it only your kind of feelings that are real? You're beyond help, you know!

Weibo "You're beyond help, you know!" You drama queen! You're really fake, you're totally fake inside and out!

Xiaobo Why do you do this to me?

Weibo You've wasted my time.

Pause.

Piling noise comes through the window clearly.

Weibo   I've wasted all these thoughts on you –

Xiaobo   Don't talk like you're in love / with me.

Weibo   You destroyed it all in one night! –

Xiaobo   You're the greatest, the greatest in the world.

Weibo   What am I to you? Your servant? You wasted my time, wasted my feelings, and cost me my closest friend!

Xiaobo   What the fuck has that got to do with me?

Weibo   Linlin won't talk to me. She used to look at me with her full attention –

Xiaobo   You're thinking too much –

Weibo   I don't even get to see her. She doesn't reply to my texts. I don't know what you said to her or what she said to you. I've only got one friend in the world, only her! You really do suck every last drop from me, every last fucking drop! Every – last – fucking – drop!

Weibo *wheezes as if he's about to get an asthma attack.*

Xiaobo   Fine, fine, I now understand. . .

Pause.

Xiaobo   You are jealous of me.

The wall clock falls and smashes into pieces.

Piling noise afar becomes a strong, pulsating rhythm, as if the flat will crumble any moment.

Pause.

Dabo *finds a package wrapped in newspaper under* **Weibo's** *bed.*

He sits down and slowly tears off the wrapping.

Xiaobo Let's be plain. You – are – jealous – of – me.

Weibo . . .

Xiaobo I know you really want to punch me . . .

Weibo . . .

Xiaobo It's all right, we'll go outside.

Weibo . . .

Xiaobo I can tell you again.

Weibo . . .

Xiaobo You said she's your best friend?

Weibo . . .

Xiaobo You know what your best friend says about you?

Weibo . . .

Xiaobo You really think she didn't know you want to shag her?

A gust of wind rattles the door.

Weibo . . .

Xiaobo Aren't you a man?

The pizza dartboard and the newspaper cut-outs fall from the wall.

Weibo . . .

Xiaobo She said . . .

Weibo . . .

Xiaobo You are a lech.

Weibo . . .

Xiaobo A perv with no balls.

The pulsating piling sound disappears.

Smack! **Dabo** *pulls out a vegetable knife and a large fruit knife from the package and slams them hard onto the table.*

At this very same moment, all three beds collapse.

Pause.

The left- and right-hand walls collapse too.

Stillness reigns.

Dabo *picks up the toilet roll from the table and goes into the bathroom.*

Silence. Half a minute passes.

Two loud bangs come from the bathroom.

The bathroom door is kicked open.

The toilet roll is kicked into the living room.

Dabo *comes out with the toilet bowl in his arms.*

He walks slowly to the table, slams the bowl on the floor. Smack! He slaps the toilet lid shut.

The central wall collapses at that same moment. In the darkness far, far away, a gigantic toilet bowl appears, tall and erect like a skyscraper.

Dabo *sits on the toilet, lights a cigarette and sucks hard.*

Silence.

He picks up the vegetable knife, hands it to **Weibo**. *No response.*

He hands it to **Xiaobo**. *No response either.*

He stabs both knives into the table and leaves them standing.

He slowly stands up, opens the lid. The giant toilet far, far away mirrors his action.

He picks up the book, the toilet roll, the beer bottles and the pen from the floor and, as he speaks, he throws them one by one into the giant toilet in the distance. Water splashes out.

Dabo *(nonchalantly)* Honestly, there's nothing I didn't know. You think I didn't know that you never thought of paying me back? – You think it didn't cross my mind that you never went to university? – You think I didn't know that you both think I'm a daft cunt? – You think I didn't know that I'm coarse? – You think I didn't know that people these days are way fucking more coarse than me? – Since I came to this city, I slowly realised, you don't need knowledge or education to make it, you only need two words – brutal and cunt. People don't work things out any more, just be a brutal cunt and walk all over everyone, save them sobs and tears. There're only two types of people in the world, brutal cunts and daft cunts. You, what kinda cunts are you? The other day, I went out bright and early at eight with five ton and drove two hours to that research place. Got the contract and my ID out for the boy at the desk. He didn't even look and asked, "Degree cert?" I asked him what cert? He said, "Are you fucking stupid? Blind, eh? It says on the contract that you need proof of a university degree. Didn't you fucking see that?" So I dashed back to Hongkeng to get a degree from the market, by the time I got back it was after one. It was 40 degrees outside and the heat cooked me through. Again the boy didn't even bother to look and chucked the cert back at me saying, "Oi, old man, how old are you? Did you fucking read the thing? Under 35, you daft cunt!" So I braved the sun and dashed back again for a new ID saying I was born in the 80s, by the time I got there again it was past five. The kid was probably still asleep, he looked at the ID then looked at me, "Fecking old sod, are you fucking stupid? Got Alzheimer's? Go to the psychiatric ward!" So I got to . . . got back here, sitting around dazed for a fucking long, long time . . . a phone call snapped me out. I asked who's there, it's just dead quiet . . . "You! It's you, isn't it? Why did you run away? Are you having a really tough time? Just tell me. No one is forcing you to study. No need to take the exam again, you don't need to. Once I've made some money I'll send you abroad! Who said my daughter isn't important? Who said that? The whole world is full of daft cunts, you're not one of them! It doesn't matter if all the world's brutal cunts are coming at you, I'll be the daft cunt! It doesn't matter if there're no daft cunts in your world, I'll be him!" "Erm, sir, sorry, we are Xingya Bank's interest-free, multi-installment, quick and easy loan services . . ."

Xiaobo's *phone rings on the table.*

Dabo *grabs the phone and throws it into the giant toilet. Then he throws the knives in.*

He picks up the card from the table.

Dabo   *(in Mandarin)* "As long as you are willing, as long as you believe."

He burns the card and throws it into the toilet bowl by the table.

A roaring flame shoots up.

A loud flush.

~ The End ~

香港藝術節簡介

香港藝術節成立於 1972 年，為國際藝壇重要的表演藝術節之一。每年均帶來約 170 場由本地、亞洲和世界頂尖藝人及團隊精心製作的表演。藝術節的節目色色俱備，既顧及古典傳統口味，亦具備新穎創意和香港難得一見的表演形式，每屆入場觀眾人次超越 150,000，其中藝術節青少年之友會員佔 19,000 人次。近年，藝術節與亞洲區內其他藝術節積極合作，孕育新作，與享譽國際的藝術機構聯合委約全新作品，並支持不同領域的藝術家進行跨區跨媒體的合作。經過 40 年的發展，今天的藝術節不論在表演藝人數目、演出水平、節目種類各方面，均為本地藝壇之最。

The Hong Kong Arts Festival

The Hong Kong Arts Festival, first established in 1972, presents some 170 performances and events by top international, regional, national and local talent during February and March every year. The eclectic mix of classical and contemporary works cater to an audience of over 150,000 including 19,000 participants of the Festival's Young Friends Scheme. The Festival also commissions, produces and publishes new works independently or in collaboration with international partners. Festival information is available at www.hk.artsfestval.org.

出版 Published by：香港藝術節協會有限公司 Hong Kong Arts Festival Society Limited

職員 Staff

行政總監 Executive Director
何嘉坤 Tisa Ho

節目 PROGRAMME

節目總監 Programme Director
梁掌瑋 Grace Lang

副節目總監 Associate Programme Director
蘇國雲 So Kwok-wan

節目經理 Programme Manager
葉健鈴 Linda Yip

外展經理 Outreach Manager
梁偉然 Ian Leung

助理製作經理 Assistant Production Manager
蘇雪凌 Shirley So

節目主任 Programme Officer
李家穎 Becky Lee

市場推廣 MARKETING

市場總監 Marketing Director
鄭尚榮 Katy Cheng

市場經理 Marketing Managers
周　怡 Alexia Chow
鍾穎茵 Wendy Chung
葉愛莉 Elly Yip

助理市場經理（票務）
Assistant Marketing Manager (Ticketing)
梁彩雲 Eppie Leung

發展 DEVELOPMENT

發展總監 Development Director
余潔儀 Flora Yu

發展經理 Development Manager
嚴翠930 Josephine Yim

助理發展經理 Assistant Development Manager
陳艷馨 Eunice Chan

會計 ACCOUNTS

會計經理 Accounting Manager
陳綺敏 Katharine Chan

助理會計經理 Assistant Accounting Manager
鄒智峯 Andy Chau

會計文員 Accounts Clerk
黃國愛 Bonia Wong

行政 ADMINISTRATION

行政秘書 Executive Secretary
陳詠詩 Heidi Chan

接待員／初級秘書
Receptionist / Junior Secretary
李美娟 Virginia Li

職員（合約）Staff (contract)

節目 PROGRAMME

物流及接待經理 Logistics Manager
金學忠 Elvis King

製作經理 Production Manager
廖卓良 Liu Cheuk-leung

節目經理 Programme Manager
梁頌怡 Kitty Leung

助理節目經理 Assistant Programme Managers
邱慧芝 Janel Yau
余瑞婷 Susanna Yu

助理監製 Assistant Producer
李宛虹 Lei Yuen-hung

外展統籌 Outreach Coordinator
陳韻婷 Alyson Chan

外展助理 Outreach Assistants
陳慧晶 Ainslee Chan
陳瑞堃 Chan Sui Kwan

項目經理 Project Manager
林淦鈞 Lam Kam Kwan

項目助理 Project Assistants
鄧詠文 Carmina Tang
林　晨 Mimi Lam

特別項目統籌 Special Project Coordinator
巫敏星 Maria Mo

藝術家統籌經理 Head Artist Coordinator
陳韻妍 Vanessa Chan

技術統籌 Technical Coordinators
黎春成 Anthony Lai
陳寶愉 Bobo Chan
陳曉楓 Chan Hiu Fung
陳詠杰 Chan Wing-kit
陳佩儀 Claudia Chan
蕭健邦 Leo Siu
何美蓮 Meilin Ho

出版 PUBLICATION

編輯 Editor
鄺潔冰 Cabbie Kwong

英文編輯 English Editor
黃進之 Nicolette Wong

助理編輯 Assistant Editor
曾逸林 Zeng Yilin

編輯助理 Editorial Assistant
伍穎妍 Winnie Ng

市場推廣 MARKETING

助理市場經理 Assistant Marketing Manager
梁愷樺 Anthea Leung

市場主任 Marketing Officer
張凱璇 Carla Cheung

票務主任 Ticketing Officer
葉晉菁 Ip Chun-ching

票務助理 Ticketing Assistant
關愷霖 Kwan Hoi-lam

客戶服務主任 Customer Services Officers
陳昕穎 Chan Yan-wing
馮敏怡 Merrie Fung
楊妙思 Iris Yeung
容巧欣 Rachel Yung

發展 DEVELOPMENT

發展經理 Development Manager
蘇啟泰 Alex So

發展助理 Development Assistant
黃苡姍 Iris Wong

行政 ADMINISTRATION

辦公室助理 Office Assistant
江宇麒 Kong Yu-ki

督印人 Publisher	何嘉坤 Tisa Ho
主編 Editor	蘇國雲 So Kwok-wan
執行編輯 Executive Editor	鄺潔冰 Cabbie Kwong
助理編輯 Assistant Editor	李宛虹 Lei Yuen-hung
平面設計 排版 Designer	梁佩琼 Polly Leung
出版 Published by	香港藝術節協會有限公司 Hong Kong Arts Festival Society Limited
印刷 Printer	稜創意有限公司 Prism Creation Ltd.
版次 Edition	2013 年 3 月初版 1st edition in March 2013
書號 / ISBN	978-988-16056-3-4
定價 / Price	港幣 HK$100
版權垂詢 Copyright Enquiry	香港藝術節協會有限公司 Hong Kong Arts Festival Society Limited

香港灣仔港灣道二號 12 字樓
12/F, 2 Harbour Road, Wan Chai, Hong Kong
電話 Tel: 2824 3555
傳真 Fax: 2824 3798, 2824 3722
網頁 Website: www.hk.artsfestival.org
電郵 Email: afgen@hkaf.org